RAND ARROYO CENTER

T0108936

European Relations with Russia

Threat Perceptions, Responses, and Strategies in the Wake of the Ukrainian Crisis

Stephanie Pezard, Andrew Radin, Thomas S. Szayna,
F. Stephen Larrabee

Prepared for the United States Army

For more information on this publication, visit www.rand.org/t/RR1579

Library of Congress Cataloging-in-Publication Data is available for this publication.
ISBN: 978-0-8330-9637-1

Published by the RAND Corporation, Santa Monica, Calif.
© Copyright 2017 RAND Corporation
RAND® is a registered trademark.

Support RAND
Make a tax-deductible charitable contribution at
www.rand.org/giving/contribute

www.rand.org

Preface

This is the second in a series of reports on the impact and implications of the Ukraine crisis on European security; it was produced under a project titled, "Security in Europe in the Wake of the Ukraine Crisis: Implications for the U.S. Army." This report examines how European states perceive Russia's behavior in eastern and northern Europe in the wake of the Ukrainian crisis. It focuses on three key analytical questions:

- Do European states see Russia as a major security threat, and, if so, what is it that Russia might threaten?
- How have European states responded to date—either individually, through the European Union, or through the North Atlantic Treaty Organization?
- How might these policies change if Russia takes even more aggressive steps in the future?

Human Subject Protections protocols have been used in this research in accordance with the appropriate statutes and U.S. Department of Defense regulations governing Human Subject Protections. The views of sources rendered anonymous by Human Subject Protections protocols are solely their own and do not represent the official policy of the U.S. Department of Defense or the U.S. government.

Other reports in the series examine European vulnerabilities to Russian pressures, Russian capabilities, Russian operations in Crimea and eastern Ukraine, and implications for the U.S. Army. This report should be of interest to those concerned with the impact on European security of Russia's illegal annexation of Crimea and the future of the relationship between European countries and Russia. Research for this project was conducted from May to October 2015.

This research was sponsored by the Deputy Chief of Staff, G-3/5/7, U.S. Army and conducted within RAND Arroyo Center's Strategy, Doctrine, and Resources Program. RAND Arroyo Center, part of the RAND Corporation, is a federally funded research and development center sponsored by the United States Army.

The Project Unique Identification Code (PUIC) for the project that produced this document is HQD146843.

Contents

Figures and Table

Figures

Table

Summary

Russia's illegal annexation and occupation of Crimea in March 2014 and subsequent support for the insurgency in eastern Ukraine have challenged the integrity of Europe's territorial borders and confirmed after the Georgia war in 2008 that Russia could react violently to perceived challenges in what it regards as its sphere of influence. This report analyzes how several key European states perceive Russia's policy in the wake of the Ukrainian crisis. First, it examines how these European states perceive Russia's behavior and policy in eastern and northern Europe, and whether they regard Russian policy in these regions as an important security priority. Particular attention is focused on fault lines within Europe regarding threat perceptions, and whether these fault lines extend to perceptions of the North Atlantic Treaty Organization (NATO) and the United States. Second, the report analyzes responses to Russian behavior. While a number of European states generally agree that a firm response to Russian aggression is required, they are also eager to maintain channels of communication with Russia. Finally, the report examines how these European states are likely to shape their relations with Russia in the future; what existing measures they intend to keep in place; what new measures they might implement; and prospects for further NATO and European Union (EU) enlargement.

This report relies on two main sources of information. The first is a series of interviews conducted from May to October 2015 in Belgium, Estonia, France, Germany, Latvia, Poland, Sweden, and the United States with U.S. and foreign officials (including EU and NATO officials), researchers, academics, and journalists familiar with European security issues in general and the crisis in Ukraine and the tensions with Russia in particular.[1] The second is a review of open-source literature in English and other European languages.

Threat Perceptions

Perceptions of Russia as a military threat following the Ukrainian crisis differ sharply across Europe and appear to be heavily influenced by geographical proximity to Russia. Most NATO members bordering Russia regard it as potentially posing an existential threat and feel that this threat can best be addressed by the deployment of U.S. and NATO troops on their territory. European countries that share a border with Russia have been living with the possibility of a Russian invasion for the better part of their history, and this experience generally has a strong impact on how they view Russia in the context of the Ukrainian crisis—this is particularly true for the Baltic States and Poland and, to a lesser extent, Finland and Norway. Russia's neighbors are painfully aware of the military imbalance between Russian forces and their own much smaller forces and the need to offset this imbalance by support from NATO. By contrast, NATO countries that do not share a border with Russia do not see as immediate a threat from Russia and worry that permanently stationing U.S. and NATO troops on the soil of NATO's easternmost members would antagonize Russia and could risk Russian countermeasures. Most of these countries see the threat posed by the Islamic State of Iraq and the Levant[2] and increasing flows

---

[1]   Appendix A provides the numbers of interviews carried out and the discussants, as well as the type of organizations the discussants belong to. Appendix B provides the questionnaire the research team used to guide the interviews in every country visited.

[2]   The organization's name transliterates from Arabic as al-Dawlah al-Islamiyah fi al-'Iraq wa al-Sham (abbreviated as Da'ish or DAESH). In the West, it is commonly referred to as the Islamic State of Iraq and the Levant (ISIL), the Islamic State of Iraq and Syria, the Islamic State of Iraq and the Sham (both abbreviated as ISIS), or simply as the Islamic State (IS). Arguments abound as to which is the most accurate translation, but here we refer to the group as ISIL.

of migrants and refugees as more pressing concerns that, alongside the tensions with Russia, require NATO's full attention.

While Russia's neighbors see Russia as capable of and potentially willing to carry out a conventional attack against them, they do not necessarily see such an attack as likely. Officials and analysts interviewed tend to describe Russia's behavior—such as its stationing of nuclear-capable missiles in Kaliningrad and overflying Polish airspace—as "bullying," "intimidation," or "posturing" rather than an indication of an imminent invasion. A more immediate fear is that Russia could employ hybrid warfare—defined as a combination of various types of operations, from conventional to irregular or psychological warfare, to influence the domestic politics of potential target countries. Our Polish and Swedish interlocutors, for instance, were concerned about Russian propaganda in Estonia or Latvia and that Russia's attempt to influence and mobilize Russian minorities in Estonia and Latvia could exacerbate tensions in the Baltic region. With an eye on this threat, Estonia and Latvia are training their forces to respond rapidly to any provocation from Russia. While they have more effective internal security services and border guards than Ukraine had, they are also aware that Russian capabilities relative to the Baltic countries give it a time-space advantage that it could exploit in any number of scenarios.

European countries, particularly eastern NATO members, are concerned that the Alliance is ill equipped to respond to the current crisis with Russia. French and Polish officials interviewed pointed out that NATO's current decisionmaking mechanism would be inadequate, in particular, if Russia were to test Article 5 "from underneath," i.e., with actions under the threshold of conventional war or that can be "plausibly denied" by Moscow. While the NATO International Staff interviewed maintained that NATO was on a path to strengthen its capability to deter Russia's ability to threaten the security of NATO members, the current efforts may not be sufficient to bring the Alliance to the necessary level of preparedness in the face of the new Russian threat. U.S. and European officials interviewed emphasized the critical importance of U.S. leadership in NATO and recognized the importance of U.S. military presence for maintaining security in Europe. Yet, the appreciation for the U.S. role in Europe does not come without reservations, with generally positive perceptions of the United States being complicated by a legacy view of the United States as imperialist by some segments of society in several countries, such as Germany and Sweden.

Responses

European countries have adopted a broad range of measures in response to the Ukrainian crisis that include economic sanctions; economic, military, and political support for the Ukrainian government; enhanced military preparedness; reassurance measures for eastern NATO members; adaptation of the Alliance to the new security environment; increased cooperation of European non-NATO members; and measures to counter Russia's information campaign in Europe. These measures seek to not only sanction Russia for its behavior in Ukraine, but also deter it from undertaking any further aggressive moves. Most European states, however, have also been careful to keep channels of communication open with Moscow on a number of issues, from the implementation of the Minsk II agreement to counterterrorism and Syria.

That Russia's behavior requires a strong response is widely accepted by most European countries. While several countries have expressed doubts on the usefulness of sanctions, their adoption was repeatedly prolonged by consensus in spite of the 28 EU members having widely different understandings of what Russia's actions mean for their own security and suffering at various degrees from sanctions and countersanctions. Such renewals are not automatic, however, and the consensus may not hold if the situation in Ukraine stagnates. Another priority of the European Union—and another area of consensus so far—is supporting the full implementation of the Minsk II agreement and helping Ukraine reform. Additionally, countries that feel most threatened by Russia militarily have worked on improving their preparedness—such as Estonia with the May 2015 Hedgehog exercise that involved 13,000 Estonian personnel.

NATO has begun its adaptation to the new threat environment as well. At the September 2014 Wales Summit, the Alliance put emphasis on the ability to rapidly deploy forces over establishing a forward presence in the Baltics as the best way to deter Russia and provide reassurance to its eastern members. This rapid deployment capability is the Readiness Action Plan (RAP), which focuses on NATO's responsiveness in a crisis. Following the Wales Summit, NATO took several steps toward implementing the RAP to include the establishment of the Very High Readiness Joint Task Force, a brigade-size force capable of deploying in seven days, with leadership rotating among seven framework nations. NATO has also worked to speed its reaction time through a number of improvements to decisionmaking processes within the North Atlantic Council; sharing processes for intelligence assessments; and logistics and infrastructure for movement across Europe. The Alliance is also examining the possibility of giving more authority to Supreme Allied Commander Europe and other commanders.

Despite these measures, a number of NATO members wanted the Alliance to go further and contend that NATO has too little capability for high-intensity conflict, cannot respond to hybrid warfare and actions that are under the threshold of clear aggression, and lacks a doctrine on preemptive deployment of a spearhead force that could be deployed in an area of growing danger. These members see the United States as their key security provider and regard U.S. forward presence as the key response to Russian aggression. Some of the demands for greater NATO involvement were fulfilled at the Warsaw Summit in July 2016, when the Alliance announced plans to deploy four rotating multinational battalions to the Baltics as an "enhanced forward presence," and to strengthen the Alliance's capabilities for defense and deterrence against a full range of threats, from hybrid to nuclear.

With regard to Russia's strategic communication efforts and internal destabilization efforts, responses have been limited. NATO officials interviewed recognized the threat but, in general, believed that NATO would be ineffective or unable to respond, because of its limited capabilities in the area of strategic communication. This could give Russia a significant advantage, despite recent progress in establishing the NATO Centre of Excellence for Strategic Communications in Riga, for example, to share best practices among member governments and improve the Alliance's doctrine, practices, and training in this area. Meanwhile, the European Union is attempting to counter the Russian message through the creation of a strategic communication task force.

While there is agreement on a firm response to Russia's aggressive moves, most European countries have also made sure to pursue dialogue with Russia on Ukraine-related issues as well as other matters of mutual interest. The European Union, for instance, is keeping a number of communication channels open while making it clear that relations with Russia are not "business as usual." One such channel is the discussion on the consequences for Russia of the implementation of the trade component (EU-Ukraine Deep and Comprehensive Free Trade Area) of the Association Agreement with Ukraine. More generally, this emphasis on dialogue reflects a concern that an overly military response to Russia might be seen as provocative and could lead to an escalation of the conflict.

Intentions

European officials interviewed generally agreed on three key elements that shape their current relations with Russia, and which they believe will continue to do so in the near future. First, there is an understanding that relations with Russia have changed irremediably. Russian actions in Crimea and eastern Ukraine created a paradigm shift, as the crisis revealed a degree of Russian assertiveness that had not been suspected previously. Second, European officials and researchers interviewed did not expect tensions with Russia to recede anytime soon. The severity of the crisis makes for a protracted impasse, complicated further by Ukraine's difficulties in the economic and governance realms. The alternative—a political and economic collapse of Ukraine, with spillover effects on neighboring countries—represents a serious concern for Poland, in particular. Finally, future actions toward Russia will largely be influenced by Russian behavior. The full implementation of the Minsk II agreement has been generally regarded as the key benchmark that will allow European countries to relax their sanctions policy on Moscow. In spite of increasing divisions within the European Union on whether sanctions are justified, they were prolonged again in December 2016 and March 2017 as some important elements of the peace process were seen as not yet fulfilled.

A number of EU countries are working on sustaining existing measures and planning for new ones. Assistance to Ukraine appears to be one of the most consensual measures and is likely to be pursued in the future. So is, to a lesser extent, the case of sanctions. With sanctions showing an effect on Russia's economy and European countries overall facing little domestic pressure to terminate them, sanctions are likely to be further prolonged in the future unless Russia shows some goodwill in implementing the Minsk II agreement.

Support for military options is more limited. Air policing missions over the Baltics, which represent a key element of NATO's reassurance measures toward its easternmost members, were reduced in September 2015. European countries—such as France—with commitments in other theaters of operations are unlikely to significantly increase presence in the Baltics. The provision of lethal aid to Ukraine is still a generally unpopular idea in Europe. General discomfort with military options can also be seen in the debate about permanently deployed forces, which, again, garner little support outside of Poland and the Baltics. Yet, the perception that the Ukrainian crisis has irremediably altered European security perceptions—turning Russia for the foreseeable future into a competitor and potential adversary rather than a partner—has provided new impetus to the debate in several European countries on whether their defense spending is adequate to address current security threats. While the response articulated at the Warsaw Summit may still seem insufficient to some, gaining full NATO agreement on an increased forward presence is a sign of wider and greater commitment for a strengthened defensive posture. The European Union, too, is exploring potential avenues for more defense-focused measures, which could include improving its ability to provide military equipment to partner nations.

Regarding NATO's reform, officials interviewed expressed a sense that the Alliance will further develop its military response to Russia. In the immediate term, NATO will continue to develop the NATO Response Force and other measures specified in the RAP and implement the measures specified at Warsaw. One fundamental issue influencing the Alliance's future response is how costs of any deployment will be shared. Finally, several interlocutors mentioned that some issues—e.g., energy security and strategic communication—might benefit from greater cooperation between the European Union and NATO. With regard to enlargement, some of the NATO officials interviewed noted that members of the Alliance were geographically divided about decisions regarding the future accession of non-NATO members such as Georgia, Ukraine, and Moldova. While NATO officially retains its open-door policy, the more geographically western countries fear that NATO enlargement will be regarded as a provocative move by Russia and could exacerbate tensions. Eastern members, by contrast, tend to believe that admitting new members into the Alliance will strengthen deterrence against future aggression by Russia, although given gaps in the institutions of these countries, they are not prepared to bring them into the Alliance in the near future. Based on that lack of consensus, and barring some unexpected major shift in the security environment, there is no realistic near-term prospect for membership for Georgia, Ukraine, or Moldova. Meanwhile, Sweden and Finland have strengthened defense cooperation with NATO. At the Wales Summit, both countries signed Host Nation Support Agreements that will make it easier for them to host predeployed NATO forces for training and exercises. Yet, both are still far from NATO membership due to mixed support at home, the risk that Russia will see Finland's accession as an offensive measure, and the Swedish reluctance to enter NATO without Finland simultaneously taking the same step.

Prospects for EU enlargement do not seem affected by events in Ukraine. EU officials interviewed appeared confident that countries close to Russia and part of the European Neighborhood Policy would continue to seek a stronger relationship with the European Union. Yet, such prospects for enlargement already had been limited. Most EU member states suffer from some degree of "enlargement fatigue," with populations increasingly skeptical about the European Union's ability to integrate newcomers successfully in a context of crisis. Yet EU officials interviewed noted that the prospect of membership—however remote—remains the most promising lever the union can use on its eastern partners.

Conclusion

Most European countries have imposed sanctions that, in combination with other factors, have driven Russia into recession and constrained future growth prospects. They have shifted resources to buttressing Ukraine economically and supporting its reform efforts. Several countries have increased their defense spending; others have halted planned declines. The United States is also showing the lead by more than quadrupling the funds devoted to the European Reassurance Initiative in its fiscal year 2017 defense budget. NATO has begun improving its capacity to respond more quickly to future contingencies. NATO and the European Union are beginning to consider how to deal with Russian unconventional threats. Despite appeals from NATO countries on Russia's periphery, there is little support elsewhere in Europe for major deployments of NATO forces further forward or arming Ukraine.

Tensions with Russia are also an opportunity, in the sense that reassurance measures help maintain interoperability gains between NATO partners after withdrawal from Afghanistan. Support for closer ties with NATO is also increasing in Sweden and Finland.

There is a clear geographical divide between countries bordering Russia and others on how real and immediate the Russian threat is, and the refugee crisis is pushing the Russian threats further into the background for numerous NATO countries. Nevertheless, the various scenarios and contingencies that we heard in Sweden, Estonia, Latvia, and Poland concerning Russian actions and potential NATO reactions need to be assessed seriously by the U.S. Department of Defense (DoD). These include

- a serious look at Russian capabilities to politically subvert a Baltic State, including the seizure of a border enclave or fomenting internal unrest. DoD could use political-military games to understand the potential Alliance difficulties in reaching consensus, the options open to NATO, and the time required. More-detailed assessment of the Baltic internal security forces and their ability to deal with potential subversion contingencies also would be valuable.

- a better understanding of the Russian ability to prevent reinforcement to the Baltic States; DoD could subject some of the "unusual" scenarios, such as the seizure of Gotland, to modeling and simulation. Similarly, for sustained air operations over the Baltic States, how important does access to Swedish (and possibly Finnish) airspace become?
- a clear view of the role that Kaliningrad might play, with its strong antiair defenses; how would NATO neutralize it?
- support for improving intelligence sharing and decisionmaking within NATO to improve indicators and warnings of Russian activity.
- looming above all of this: the nuclear issue. How might escalation be controlled, and what would be the levers available?

Basically, the ball is now in the Russian court. If Moscow deescalates the Ukraine crisis, or there is no increase in fighting, most European governments will be sympathetic to some relaxation of sanctions. If, on the other hand, Russia escalates its involvement in Ukraine, or threatens aggressive steps elsewhere, the debate in Europe about a further response will be renewed. Russia may also be playing for time, knowing that there is a clear geographical divide between countries bordering Russia and others on how real and immediate the Russian threat is, and the migration crisis is pushing concerns about a Russian threat even further into the background for many European countries.

The threat of international and domestic terrorism, the Syrian and Libyan civil wars, and the unprecedented flood of refugees are all powerful distractions that tend to dominate the concerns of all but Russia's closest neighbors. Nevertheless, the Ukraine crisis has caused the Alliance to refocus its attention on the defense of NATO territory for the first time in more than 20 years. This refocus should continue to yield gradual improvements in the Alliance's defensive capabilities, even as the prospects for concerted Western action in distant out-of-area contingencies continue to diminish.

Acknowledgments

We are grateful for the support of many individuals over the course of this research project. We would like to express our sincere thanks to Timothy Muchmore for initiating and supporting this project. This research would not have been possible without the many individuals—in Belgium, Estonia, France, Germany, Latvia, Poland, Sweden, and the United States—who took the time to share with us their insights on European security and politics, providing invaluable input to this report. We would also like to thank Ethan Corbin, Arnaud Guillois, Andres Kasekamp, Andrew Michta, and Marco Overhaus, who facilitated some of these discussions.

A number of other people helped make this study possible. Olga Oliker played a key role in the leadership of this project. We thank Christopher Chivvis, Steven Flanagan, and Andrew Weiss for their helpful comments on an earlier draft of this report. Finally, our thanks also go to Natalie Ziegler and Samantha Bennett for providing editing support.

Abbreviations

CDU	Christian Democratic Union
CSDP	Common Security and Defense Policy
DCFTA	Deep and Comprehensive Free Trade Area
EEAS	European External Action Service
EU	European Union
IDC	Institut de la démocratie et de la coopération
ISIL	Islamic State of Iraq and the Levant
MFA	Ministry of Foreign Affairs
MP	member of parliament
NATO	North Atlantic Treaty Organization
NORDEFCO	Nordic Defence Cooperation
NRF	NATO Response Force
OSCE	Organization for Security and Cooperation in Europe
RAP	Readiness Action Plan (NATO)
SACEUR	Supreme Allied Commander Europe
SHAPE	Supreme Headquarters Allied Powers Europe
SIPRI	Stockholm International Peace Research Institute
SPD	Sozialdemokratische Partei Deutschlands (German Social Democrat Party)
VJTF	Very High Readiness Joint Task Force (NATO)

CHAPTER ONE

Introduction

Overview

Russia's illegal annexation and occupation of Crimea in March 2014 and subsequent support for the insurgency in eastern Ukraine have challenged not only the integrity of Europe's territorial borders, but also its security environment. The Georgia war in 2008 had already shown that Russia could react violently to perceived challenges in the former Soviet space, in spite of cooperation efforts such as the creation of the Russia–North Atlantic Treaty Organization (NATO) Council in 2002. Russia's actions again showed its willingness to use force to change existing territorial boundaries and raised increasing questions about the possibility of future Russian aggression.[1] While the RAND Corporation's report *Russia and the West After the Ukrainian Crisis: European Vulnerabilities to Russian Pressures*[2] examined what avenues Russia may have at its disposal to harm European countries on various levels (militarily, economically, politically), this report analyzes how several key European states perceive the Russian threat. It addresses

---

[1]   In this report, unless otherwise noted, we use "Europe" and "Europeans" to refer to the states of the European Union and NATO members other than the United States and Canada. In using this shorthand, we do not mean to imply that other countries with all or some of their territory on the European continent (including Russia, Ukraine, Moldova, and Belarus), are not "European."

[2]   F. Stephen Larrabee, Stephanie Pezard, Andrew Radin, Nathan A. Chandler, Keith W. Crane, and Thomas S. Szayna, *Russia and the West After the Ukrainian Crisis: European Vulnerabilities to Russian Pressures*, Santa Monica, Calif.: RAND Corporation, RR-1305-A, 2017.

three specific questions: (1) Do these Europeans see Russia as a major security threat? (2) What is it that Russia might threaten? And (3) What responses have they devised so far, and what might they do if Russian behavior becomes even more assertive in the future?

Approach

This report relies on two main sources of information. First, we conducted a series of semistructured interviews from May to October 2015 in Belgium, Estonia, France, Germany, Latvia, Poland, Sweden, and the United States with U.S. and foreign officials (including EU and NATO officials[3]), researchers, academics, and journalists familiar with European security issues in general, and the crisis in Ukraine and the tensions with Russia in particular. The goal of these interviews was to gauge the different perceptions within these countries of the major threat posed by Russia. In a few instances, this study also draws from interviews conducted in Ukraine for other RAND studies between April and August 2015. Appendix A provides the numbers of interviews carried out, as well as the type of organizations with which the discussants were affiliated.[4] Appendix B provides the questionnaire the research team used to guide the interviews in every country visited. The choice of countries visited—Belgium, Estonia, France, Germany, Latvia, Poland, Sweden[5]—was based on several considerations, including the following: countries that have played a noticeable diplomatic role in the Ukraine crisis; former Soviet and non–former Soviet countries; NATO and non-NATO states; and countries that share and do not share a border with Russia. The study team also wanted to gather input from the two key international organizations that have been involved in the lead-up to and the consequences of the Ukraine

---

[3]   Conversations with EU officials were with European External Action Service (EEAS) officials, unless otherwise stated. Conversations with NATO officials were with NATO International Staff officials, unless otherwise stated.

[4]   More-detailed information about the organizations and the discussants' positions are not provided so as to protect their anonymity.

[5]   In addition to the United States.

crisis—NATO and the European Union. Finally, constraints in terms of time and resources prevented the study team from extending its visits beyond the seven countries mentioned above.

The interviews were supplemented by the second source of data: a review of select open-source literature in English and other European languages. Another report from this project, Larrabee et al., 2017, provides more-detailed information on European relations with Russia—in terms of financial, trade, and energy dependency, but also with regard to public opinion views of Russia. While both reports can be read independently, the reader will find that they collectively paint a more complete picture of Europe's complex relationship with Russia in the wake of the Ukraine crisis.

Organization of This Report

Chapter Two examines how several key European states perceive Russia's behavior in eastern and northern Europe—and what it means for them. Is Russia perceived as a threat, and, if so, what type of threat is it (e.g., military, economic, internal)? Most importantly, how does Russia compare with other strategic priorities? This chapter highlights fault lines within Europe with regard to threat perceptions and examines whether European and U.S. perceptions align or differ. It also examines whether perceptions of NATO and the United States have evolved as a consequence of the Ukraine crisis. Chapter Three analyzes the responses of Europeans to Russian behavior in Ukraine. In spite of increasing divisions, particularly on the issue of economic sanctions toward Russia, Europeans generally agree that Russia's behavior requires a firm response yet are also eager to maintain channels of communication with Moscow. Chapter Four examines European intentions regarding how to pursue their relationship with Russia in the future; what existing measures they intend to keep in place and what new measures they might implement; and what the prospects are for NATO enlargement as well as for the EU Neighborhood Policy (ENP). A concluding chapter provides some implications of European perceptions, responses, and intentions for U.S. policy.

CHAPTER TWO

Perceptions

Perceptions of Russia in the wake of the Ukrainian crisis differ sharply across Europe. A critical factor influencing European perceptions of the military threat posed by Russia appears to be geographical proximity to Russia.[1] Most NATO members bordering Russia perceive an existential threat that they feel can be addressed only through the presence of U.S. and NATO troops on their territory.[2] With the exception of Romania, whose views of Russia are closer to those of Poland and the Baltic States, NATO's western and southern members do not see as immediate a threat from Russia and fear that too forceful a NATO response would not only be unnecessarily expensive, but would also risk provoking Russia and further exacerbating tensions with Moscow. Most of these countries see the Islamic State of Iraq and Levant (ISIL) and increasing flows of migrants and refugees as more pressing concerns that, together with the tensions with Russia, require NATO's full attention.[3]

---

[1] Many NATO officials explained that geography was a reliable shorthand for understanding different countries' perspectives (interviews with NATO officials, June 16 and 17, 2015). A similar point was made during the following interviews: interview with French officials, June 18, 2015; interview with French officials, May 12, 2015; interview with EU official, June 10, 2015. This individual also noted that the same geographic distinction applies to EU officials: Even though they feel "European" and try to be neutral, those closer to Russia by citizenship tend to see Russia as a threat more than their colleagues do.

[2] Interviews with Estonian, Latvian, and Polish officials, July 13–17, 2015.

[3] Interviews with NATO officials, June 16 and 17, 2015.

Threat Perceptions of a Russian Conventional Attack

European countries that share a border with Russia (see Figure 2.1) have lived with the possibility of a Russian invasion for the better part of their history. In all of these countries, perceptions of current relations with Russia are heavily influenced by a legacy of Russian domination and occupation, not only during the Soviet period but stretching back into the years of czarist rule. Negative bilateral images persist in many of these countries at the popular level, and even if those perceptions are not reflected at all or to the same extent at the elite level, they affect the political discourse in these countries. Those historically rooted perceptions influence how they view Russia in the context of the Ukrainian crisis.

One Finnish official noted that Russia is Finland's No. 1 security concern ("and will always be") for historical reasons.[4] The incorporation of Finland into the Russian empire during the 19th century, the securing of Finnish independence only by force of arms in 1918, the Soviet invasion and attempted annexation of Finland in 1939–1940, renewed Finish-Soviet hostilities in 1941–1944 as an offshoot of Nazi Germany's attack on the Soviet Union, and the constraints on Finnish sovereignty that Moscow imposed during the Cold War remain important factors that continue to influence Finnish perceptions of Russia. Similarly, Stalin's forceful annexation of the Baltic States and their incorporation into the Soviet Union as a consequence of the pact signed between Germany and the Soviet Union in 1939 strongly color the security perceptions and attitudes toward Russia in Lithuania, Latvia, and Estonia. Russia's role in the partition of Poland in the late 18th century, which resulted in Poland's loss of sovereignty for more than a century, and then the history of Polish-Soviet conflict and the Soviet forceful incorporation of Poland into its sphere of influence after World War II is deeply ensconced in the Polish political discourse.

Notwithstanding the Polish-Russian 2011–2013 rapprochement, studies of contemporary media portrayals of Russia and Poland in each

---

[4]   Interview with Finnish official, July 14, 2015.

Figure 2.1
Map of Europe

SOURCE: Central Intelligence Agency, *World FactBook*, website, undated.

RAND *RR1579-2.1*

country indicate that the nationalist and historicist biases continue to influence their relations.[5]

Russian officials tend to quickly dismiss the security concerns of their western neighbors as solely driven by anti-Russian biases that persist in these countries. For example, academic and activist Sergei Markov cautioned Finland against considering NATO membership out of such supposed nationalistic biases:

> Finland should think of the consequences, if it ponders joining NATO. It must ask: could joining start World War III? . . . Russophobia can start a third world war. Finland is one of the most Russophobic countries in Europe, after Sweden, Poland and the Baltic countries.[6]

Even in Norway, with its short Norwegian-Russian border in the Arctic region, Russia continues to be one of the defining elements of Norway's security policy that prompted it to join NATO in the early days of the Cold War. Although Norway has enjoyed cordial relations with Russia over the past few years, particularly after the resolution of the territorial dispute in the Barents Sea in 2010,[7] Russia's illegal annex-

---

[5]   In her study of media portrayal of each other in Poland and Russia, Ekaterina Levintova notes that

> Historically, Polish public discourse presented Russia as a despotic, barbaric, autocratic and aggressive country, antithetical to European values, and its subjects as uneducated, unrefined, slavish, violent, unreliable and prone to excessive drinking. The relations between the two countries were portrayed in terms of an assault by barbaric Russia on civilised and European Poland.

Similarly, in Russian media, Poles are often portrayed as "sly, treacherous, proud, boastful, condescending, rebellious, anti-Russian and fanatical" (Ekaterina Levintova, "Good Neighbours? Dominant Narratives About the 'Other' in Contemporary Polish and Russian Newspapers," *Europe-Asia Studies*, Vol. 62, No. 8, 2010, pp. 1339–1361).

[6]   Comments by Russian President Vladimir Putin's senior political adviser, Sergei Markov, to Swedish and Finnish media, as reported in Gerard O'Dwyer, "Russia Warns Sweden and Finland Against NATO Membership," *Defense News*, June 12, 2014.

[7]   Walter Gibbs, "Russia and Norway Reach Accord on Barents Sea," *New York Times*, April 27, 2010. The agreement gave Norway an additional 54,000 square miles of continental shelf and binds the two countries into working jointly to exploit cross-border oil and gas deposits (U.S. Energy Information Administration, "Norway," database, updated April 28, 2014).

ation and occupation of Crimea has caused growing concerns about its intentions among the Norwegian public.[8] An April 2015 Gallup poll reveals that Norwegian disapproval of the actions of Russia's leadership is greater than in nine other countries surveyed.[9]

Security concerns of Russia's western neighbors are also based on strategic considerations. In case of a Russian-inspired conflict in the Baltic States, Polish territory could become a strategic corridor for NATO and an area of combat operations because of proximity to Russian military bases in Kaliningrad and, possibly in the future, Belarus (if Russia can persuade Belarus authorities to allow such installations).[10] Russia has extensive anti-access/area denial capabilities, including long-range antiair and antiship missile, based in Kaliningrad. These capabilities allow Russia to constrain or at least delay the deployment of NATO forces by air or sea to the Baltic States.[11]

Russia's western neighbors are also painfully aware of the military imbalance between their own forces and Russia's unless they receive NATO—and particularly U.S.—reinforcement. In conditions of a hypothetical Russian conventional attack, officials from Estonia and Latvia argued that Russian capabilities relative to the Baltic countries gave Russia a time-space advantage that Russia could exploit in any number of scenarios.[12] Officials from both Baltic States estimated that

---

[8] Interview with Norwegian officials, July 14, 2015.

[9] Eight-nine percent disapprove, ahead of (among Nordic countries) 86 percent in Finland and 82 percent in Sweden (2014 Gallup poll cited in Jon Clifton, "Russia Receives Lowest Approval in World; U.S. Highest," Gallup website, April 21, 2015).

[10] Interview with Polish officials, July 14, 2015. As of 2015, Russia did not have any military bases yet in Belarus but had started talks with Belarus to establish an air base on its territory. See Yaras Karmanau, "Putin Moves to Establish Russian Military Base in Belarus," Associated Press, September 19, 2015; and "Belarus Says Does Not Need a Russian Military Base: Report," Reuters, October 6, 2015.

[11] Interviews with U.S. and Swedish officials, discussions with U.S. and European think tank analysts, July 2015 and February 2016; David A. Shlapak and Michael Johnson, *Reinforcing Deterrence on NATO's Eastern Flank: Wargaming the Defense of the Baltics*, Santa Monica, Calif.: RAND Corporation, RR-1253-A, 2016.

[12] Recent RAND analysis supports this assessment of a Russian time-space advantage. See David Ochmanek, Andrew R. Hoehn, James T. Quinlivan, Seth G. Jones, and Edward L. Warner, *America's Security Deficit: Addressing the Imbalance Between Strategy and Resources*

they would have very little reaction time in a crisis. One Latvian official, for example, assessed the warning time for a conventional attack to be only 48 to 72 hours, while a former official—also from Latvia—hypothesized a scenario in which Russian airborne forces could seize Riga with virtually no warning.[13] Finally, Russia's "snap" exercises—such as a July 2013 exercise in which 160,000 troops were deployed in less than 72 hours—have raised concerns in Poland, especially as NATO is lacking the ability to rapidly deploy substantial ground forces.[14] Out of nine countries surveyed in early 2015 by the Pew Research Center, Poland showed the greatest concern about Russia, with 70 percent of those surveyed considering it to be, militarily, a "major threat" to its neighbors (see Figure 2.2).[15]

Conversely, the countries whose populations are less inclined to see Russia as a threat to its neighbors (Figure 2.3) tend to be either countries from southern Europe, such as Italy, with other strategic concerns than Russia, or countries where pacifist opinion is prominent, such as Germany. These countries are also least likely to blame Russia for the violence in eastern Ukraine: 29 percent in Italy and Germany see Russia as being "most to blame," in contrast to 44 percent in France and 57 percent in Poland.[16]

Yet, the fact that Russia is seen as capable and potentially willing to carry out a conventional attack against its neighbors does not mean that such an attack is seen as likely. Polish and Finnish officials and analysts interviewed tended to describe Russia's behavior—such

---

in a Turbulent World, Santa Monica, Calif.: RAND Corporation, RB-9870-RC, 2015, pp. 5–8; and Shlapak and Johnson, 2016.

[13] Interviews with Estonian and Latvian officials and former Latvian official, July 15 and 17, 2015.

[14] Interviews with Polish officials, July 13, 2015; Bruce Jones, "Russia Places 38,000 Troops on Alert for Snap Exercises," *Jane's Defence Weekly*, March 16, 2015.

[15] Katie Simmons, Bruce Stokes, and Jacob Poushter, "NATO Publics Blame Russia for Ukrainian Crisis, but Reluctant to Provide Military Aid," Pew Research Center, June 2015, p. 51. Other possible responses were "minor threat" or "not a threat."

[16] Simmons, Stokes, and Poushter, 2015, p. 52. Other possible responses were "pro-Russian separatists in Ukraine," "Ukrainian government," "Western countries, such as those in Europe and the U.S.," "more than one named," "all of the above," or "none of the above."

Figure 2.2
Percentage of Opinion That Considers Russia a Major Military Threat to Its Neighboring Countries (Spring 2015)

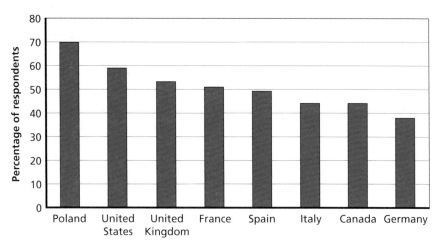

SOURCE: Simmons, Stokes, and Poushter, 2015, p. 51.
RAND *RR1579-2.2*

Figure 2.3
Percentage of Opinion That Considers Russia Not a Military Threat to Its Neighboring Countries (Spring 2015)

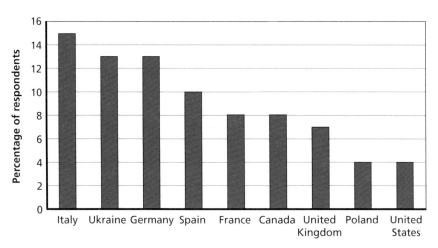

SOURCE: Simmons, Stokes, and Poushter, 2015, p. 51.
RAND *RR1579-2.3*

as the stationing of nuclear-capable missiles in Kaliningrad and over-flights over Polish airspace—as "bullying," "intimidation," or "posturing" rather than as indication that Russia is seriously planning an invasion.[17] In Poland, a large-scale conventional war is seen as possible but unlikely. As one Polish official put it, "Russia is ready but not suicidal."[18] Interlocutors in Estonia and Latvia contended that Putin would be unlikely to take military action against the Baltic States as long as the war in Ukraine continued. Officials interviewed recognized that Russian interests in Ukraine are greater than those in the Baltic States.[19] Some Baltic officials speculated that the most likely period when conflict might begin would be two to three years in the future, as the increasing pressure on the Russian budget from declining oil prices would begin to have a strong impact on the Russian economy, although this view was not universally held.[20]

Sweden, too, has signaled that it takes the Russian threat seriously, even if Swedish officials do not foresee any immediate threat of attack against the Nordic countries.[21] The Swedish defense bill for 2016–2020, which represents a consensus view of the country's shifting defense priorities, highlights Russian aggression in Ukraine and the possibility of further aggression in the future. Sweden has also sought to strengthen its bilateral and multilateral cooperation. In particular, it has used its leadership of the Nordic Defense Cooperation (NORDE-FCO) group in 2014 to press for a stronger defense against potential Russian aggression in the region.[22]

Sweden does not share a land border with Russia, but some in Sweden see parts of Swedish territory, such as the strategically located

---

[17]   Interview with Polish officials, July 14, 2015; interview with Polish analysts, July 14, 2015; interview with Finnish official, May 28, 2015.

[18]   Interview with Polish officials, July 13, 2015.

[19]   Interviews with Estonian and Latvian officials, July 15 and 17, 2015.

[20]   Interviews with Estonian and Latvian officials, July 15 and 17, 2015.

[21]   Interviews with Swedish officials and think tank analysts, July 20 and 21, 2015.

[22]   Gerard O'Dwyer, "Sweden Proposes Aggressive Nordic Defense," *Defense News*, February 10, 2015a.

Gotland Island, as vulnerable to a potential Russian attack.[23] According to this line of thought, Russian seizure and consequent installation of surface-to-air missiles on Gotland would allow Russia to control airspace over the central Baltic Sea and constrain U.S. and NATO quick access to and reinforcement of the Baltic States. The scenario envisions a preemptive Russian attack in the context of a conflict over the Baltic States in order to reduce the likelihood of a NATO response.[24] Some interlocutors noted the significant questions about the plausibility of a Russian attack on Gotland, opined that the defense of Gotland has significant political resonance, and observed that the suggestion of the scenario may be intended to address diminished Swedish defense spending.[25] Gotland's strategic value is also diminished by the fact that Russia already has significant long-range air defense capabilities over the central Baltic Sea based in Kaliningrad.[26] In any event, although Sweden is not a NATO member, a direct attack against Swedish territory would likely provoke a strong reaction by NATO members and eliminate any ambiguity about Russian intentions.

One way to interpret the Swedish discussions about the defense of Gotland is to see the island as a surrogate for Sweden's defense concerns more generally. The growing concern about the weakness of the defenses on the island is a sign of increasing concern about Sweden's overall defensive capabilities in general. Indeed, the discussion about the island takes place in the context of a larger debate on reversing the decline in Swedish defense spending.[27]

---

[23] Interviews with two different Swedish think tank analysts, July 20, 2015.

[24] Interview with Swedish think tank analyst, July 21, 2015.

[25] Interviews with two different Swedish think tank analysts, July 20, 2015.

[26] Interview with Swedish think tank analyst, July 21, 2015. Regardless of the island's military value, the capacity of Sweden to defend it is politically important, as it signals the extent of the country's overall defense capacity. While substantial numbers of Swedish troops were present on the island during the Cold War, its subsequent demilitarization is seen by many in Sweden as a sign of the country's declining military capabilities (interviews with Swedish think tank analysts and journalists, July 20, 2015).

[27] Interviews with Swedish think tank analysts, July 20 and 21, 2015.

Just as in Sweden and Poland, in Finland there is a perception of higher risk but not necessarily a military threat from Russia. One Finnish official noted that the Russian Army is much smaller than it was during the Soviet era and, as a result, does not elicit the same fears in Finland as it used to. The level of international tension is also considerably lower than during the Cold War. This official did not feel that Finland is militarily threatened, and Russia's aggressive or disruptive actions in Nordic countries, such as overflights or the suspected presence of submarines, are mostly seen as posturing and provocations rather than as an indication of future aggression.[28] The potential rationale for Russia in attacking Finland is unclear, and Russia has "other problems elsewhere," from Ukraine to the Caucasus and Central Asia, that require its attention.[29]

Sharing a short border with Russia in Europe's Arctic, Norway has a more sanguine view of potential Russian threat than its eastern Nordic neighbors.[30] While it has aligned itself with EU policy on sanctions—Norwegian Prime Minister Erna Solberg publicly expressed her disapproval of Russian policy in Ukraine[31]—there is no indication that Norway expects any aggressive move from Russia against its territory. Norwegian officials interviewed underlined the fact that Norway has generally good relations with Russia.[32] Militarily, Norway's and Russia's respective Arctic military brigades have regularly engaged in joint training exercises on land and at sea on a variety of missions ranging from search and rescue to air defense.[33] At the same time, Norway has consistently sought more NATO involvement in the Arctic region—

---

[28] Interview with Finnish official, May 28, 2015.

[29] Interview with Finnish official, May 28, 2015.

[30] Andrew Higgins, "Norway Reverts to Cold War Mode as Russian Air Patrols Spike," April 1, 2015.

[31] "Russia-Norway Tensions at Liberation Ceremony," *Local*, October 25, 2014.

[32] In October 2014, in the midst of the Ukrainian crisis, Norwegian and Russian officials celebrated together the 70th anniversary of the liberation of the Finnmark region (bordering both Norway and Russia) from Nazi occupation ("Finnmark Celebrates 70-Year Liberation Anniversary," *Norway Post*, October 22, 2014).

[33] O'Dwyer, 2012.

where it shares a border with Russia—through exercises.[34] The Svalbard archipelago, too, could reemerge as a source of tension between Norway and Russia.[35] In June 2014, Norway opened a new military border post to "strengthen Norway's ability to monitor and control the Norwegian-Russian border."[36] This monitoring and efforts at preparedness are more of a traditional feature of Norwegian defense policy than a reaction to the Ukraine crisis—Norwegian officials interviewed described Norway's historical approach to security as not having been changed by the new tensions with Russia[37]—yet Russia's aggression in Ukraine, combined with lower global prices of oil, has already reduced Norwegian-Russian cooperation, particularly on energy issues.[38]

For countries on the western and southern parts of the European continent, Russia is generally not a top strategic priority. Other issues, such as the war in Syria, foreign fighters joining ISIL, and the European migrant crisis take precedence. French officials interviewed saw ISIL (and counterterrorism in general), Iran, Mali, Libya, and the migrant crisis as higher strategic priorities than Russia.[39] Even in Fin-

---

[34] Brooke Smith-Windsor, "Putting the 'N' Back in NATO: A High North Policy Framework for the Atlantic Alliance?" NATO Research Paper No. 94, July 2013, pp. 5–6.

[35] Svein Vigeland Rottem, "The Political Architecture of Security in the Arctic—The Case of Norway," *Arctic Review on Law and Politics*, Vol. 4, No. 2, 2013, pp. 249–250. The 1920 Svalbard Treaty gives Norway sovereignty over the archipelago but is silent on whether this extends to the archipelago's continental shelf and economic zone. In the past, incidents have taken place between Norwegian authorities and Russian fishing vessels in the Svalbard's economic zone (for an example, see "Norway Kicked Russian Patrol Vessels out of Spitsbergen," *Barents Observer*, May 27, 2008).

[36] Norwegian Ministry of Foreign Affairs, "Norway's Arctic Policy," 2015, p. 19.

[37] Interview with Norwegian officials, July 14, 2015.

[38] Ulf Sverdrup and Elana Wilson Rowe, "Norway Is Re-Thinking Its Russian Relations," *Europe's World*, Summer 2015.

[39] Interview with French government-affiliated think tank analyst, June 18, 2015; interview with French think tank analyst, June 19, 2015; interview with French officials, May 12, 2015; interview with French government-affiliated think tank analyst, June 19, 2015.

land, one official mentioned foreign fighters returning from Iraq and Syria as a threat on par with Russia.[40]

However, there is general concern that, even if Russia did not choose to initiate a conventional war, the risk of accidental escalation remains because of the increase in air traffic over northern Europe and the fact that Russian pilots violating NATO airspace often turn off their transponders.[41] Polish officials expressed concern that a series of errors and miscalculations might provoke a large-scale conflict.[42] The institutional mechanisms established during the Cold War to prevent such accidental escalation—particularly when the East or the West engaged in exercises—would be useful again but have been largely neglected since the end of the Cold War.[43]

Threat Perceptions of a Russian Hybrid Warfare Scenario

More Europeans are concerned about the risk of Russia employing hybrid warfare than of it carrying out a conventional attack. There is no shared agreement about the definition of what a hybrid threat constitutes, though the term appears to be best understood as a combination of various types of operations, from conventional to irregular or psychological warfare, to influence the domestic politics of target countries.[44]

---

[40] Interview with Finnish official, May 28, 2015. In January 2015, the International Centre for the Study of Radicalisation and the Munich Conference ranked Finland as the western European country with the sixth-highest estimated number of foreign fighters per capita, behind (in decreasing order) Belgium, Denmark, Sweden, France, Austria, and the Netherlands (Peter R. Neumann, "Foreign Fighters Total in Syria/Iraq Now Exceeds 20,000; Surpasses Afghanistan Conflict in the 1980s," London: International Centre for the Study of Radicalisation, January 26, 2015).

[41] For one instance over Sweden, see Simon Johnson, "Sweden Intercepts Russian Military Planes Flying with Their Transponders Off over Baltic Region," Reuters, March 24, 2015.

[42] Interview with Polish officials, July 14, 2015.

[43] Interview with French government-affiliated think tank analyst, June 18, 2015.

[44] See Frank Hoffman, "On Not-So-New Warfare: Political Warfare vs. Hybrid Threats," *War on the Rocks*, July 28, 2014; Mark Galeotti, "The 'Gerasimov Doctrine' and Russian

Our Polish interlocutors underlined that hybrid should be seen as an add-on, not an alternative to, traditional military means.[45] They were concerned in particular about Russia's propaganda in the Baltic States and its attempt to influence Russian minorities in those countries.[46] One such hybrid contingency would be a Narva separatist scenario in Estonia, which some Polish officials presented as plausible.[47] A similar scenario could involve the large Russian minority in Latgale (eastern Latvia).[48] In yet another scenario, Russia would be using other minorities in the Baltic States to attain its ends, such as the Polish minority in Lithuania, which has allied politically with the Russian minority in the face of Lithuanian measures that have targeted minority populations.[49] Polish interlocutors downplayed risks to Poland, noting that the country has neither a significant Russian minority nor pro-Russian groups.[50]

Swedish experts and policymakers, echoing others in the region, see the main military vulnerability, and most likely point of Russian aggression, to be the Baltic States.[51] They, too, see a hybrid scenario involving the apparent mobilization of Russian minorities in Estonia or Latvia as generally plausible. One researcher observed that Russia might pursue three possible "small bite" forms of aggression: a "territorial" scenario, in which Russia captures a small pro-Russian area, such as Narva in Estonia, to demonstrate the failure of Article 5; a "functional" scenario, in which Russia undertakes aggression because of some constraint on its actions, such as the closing of land transpor-

---

Non-Linear War," blog post, *In Moscow's Shadows*, July 6, 2014. For a skeptical view, see Damien Van Puyvelde, "Hybrid War—Does It Even Exist?" *NATO Review*, 2015.

[45] Interview with Polish official, July 13, 2015.

[46] Interview with Polish analysts, July 14, 2015.

[47] Interview with Polish officials, July 13, 2015.

[48] On Latgale and calls for a "Latgalian People's Republic," see Andrew Higgins, "Latvian Region Has Distinct Identity, and Allure for Russia," *New York Times*, May 20, 2015.

[49] Interview with Polish officials, July 13, 2015.

[50] Interview with Polish analysts, July 14, 2015.

[51] Interviews with Swedish officials, July 21, 2015.

tation links to Kaliningrad; and an "assets" scenario, involving Russia taking military action related to, for example, a trapped submarine or the presence of a dissident in a foreign country.[52]

German officials and analysts interviewed are concerned as well about Russian efforts at subversion and internal destabilization but tend to see hybrid warfare and the Russian threat in terms of non-violent efforts to undermine the liberal and constitutional order in Europe. A significant portion of the population in Germany sees the use of military force to achieve political objectives as obsolete, and the use or deployment of armed forces by NATO to address a military threat in the Baltics as unnecessary and inappropriate.[53] According to think tank analysts, in practice, there is very little difference between German Chancellor Angela Merkel's (Christian Democratic Union [CDU]) and Foreign Minister Frank-Walter Steinmeier's (Social Democratic Party of Germany [SPD]) views of Moscow. However, the left wing of the SPD and parts of the base still cling to views that regard Russia as a potential partner. The most concrete disagreement within the coalition, for example, appears to be about how the European Union should cooperate with the Eurasian Union, with Merkel and the CDU less open to cooperation than the SPD and Steinmeier. Growing instability in the coalition, in large part due to the migration crisis, may undermine a unified policy on Russia in the future.[54]

Estonian and Latvian analysts and officials interviewed acknowledge that Russia has more or less constantly sought to infiltrate and destabilize their countries through covert means. Estonian think tank analysts noted that Russia could easily undertake a provocation that

---

[52] Interview with Swedish think tank analyst, July 21, 2015.

[53] Interviews with German think tank analysts, discussions at conference, June 18 and 22, 2015. See Claudia Major and Christian Mölling, "A Hybrid Security Policy for Europe: Resilience, Deterrence, and Defense as Leitmotifs," *Stiftung Wissenschaft und Politik* Comments, Vol. 22, German Institute for International and Security Affairs, April 2015; Bastian Giegerich, "Workshop Report: Perspectives on Hybrid Warfare," *IISS Voices*, International Institute for Strategic Studies, July 1, 2015; and "Audio: Hybride Kriegführung—'Vielmehr als ein Hype,'" German Ministry of Defense, August 4, 2015.

[54] Interviews with German think tank analysts and academic, June 18 and 19, 2015, and February 4, 2016.

would bring Russian speakers to rally or protest, as they did in the Bronze Soldier incident in 2007.[55] One former Latvian government official suggested a possible scenario in which Russia might seek to encourage the development of a terrorist movement against the Latvian government by fabricating attacks on Russian speakers.[56] However, despite recognizing the possibility of a Russian provocation in these areas, there was doubt that Moscow's mobilization of Russian-speaking populations in the Baltic States would be sustainable. To be sure, Estonian and Latvian officials emphasized that they were monitoring Russian destabilization efforts, but they were not overly concerned that this was a major vulnerability, especially when compared with the conventional threat. A Latvian official, for example, stated that "a conventional invasion of the entire country is the big fear, not hybrid and not a limited conventional attack."[57]

Two factors may account for this apparent lack of concern regarding a hybrid threat in the Baltics. First, the Baltic countries believe that they are prepared for the threat. They are training their forces to rapidly respond to any provocation from Russia, and officials in both Estonia and Latvia have clearly stated their intention to shoot any "little green men." Their belief is that a NATO conventional deterrent, including U.S. forces and ideally with the participation of other NATO countries, will prevent Russia from escalating to protect Russian covert activity. Furthermore, as our interlocutors throughout the region argued, Estonia and Latvia have effective internal security services and border guards that are more capable of protecting their territory than the ones Ukraine had.[58] Polish researchers emphasized that

---

[55] Interviews with Estonian and Latvian officials and think tank analysts, July 15 and 17, 2015. For a good account of the Bronze Soldier incident, see Heather A. Conley, Theodore P. Gerber, Lucy Moore, and Mihaela David, *Russian Soft Power in the 21st Century: An Examination of Russian Compatriot Policy in Estonia*, Center for Strategic and International Studies, August 2011.

[56] Interview with former Latvian government official, July 15, 2015.

[57] Interviews with Estonian and Latvian officials, July 15 and 17, 2015.

[58] Although there was a perception that there is room for improvement in the preparedness of the internal security forces, especially in Latvia. Interviews with foreign officials based in Riga, July 15, 2015.

point, noting that Latvia and Estonia are well-functioning states and that would make it more difficult for Russia to achieve the same successes it had in Ukraine.[59] Estonian and Latvian officials argued that Russia's hybrid strategy in Ukraine was a failure, since, in August 2014, Russia had to escalate with well-armed conventional forces when the separatists were on the verge of defeat, and that Russia would probably not use the same strategy again.[60] Second, there may be a desire on the part of our interlocutors in the Baltic States to downplay vulnerability to the threat of subversion to avoid calling attention to the problem posed by the integration of the Russian minority. By claiming that "our" Russians are satisfied and unlikely to be manipulated by Russia, mainstream opinion in Estonia and Latvia can avoid considering the need for compromise on citizenship or language issues for the Russian minority.

Russia's Strategic Communication Efforts

Russia's influence is reinforced through its "Compatriot Policy" supporting Russian speakers in former Soviet Republics.[61] According to one think tank analyst in Riga, Russian propaganda is "undermining social integration" by encouraging unachievable demands for language and citizenship. In Latvia, one interlocutor maintained that the Russian-speaking population exists in a separate media environment; they generally have little interest in watching Latvian-language programs, since Russian programs are easier to understand and have significantly higher production values, including broadcasts of popular Western

---

[59]   Interview with Polish analyst, July 13, 2015.

[60]   Interviews with Estonian and Latvian officials, July 15 and 17, 2015. On this point, see Michael Kofman, Katya Migacheva, Brian Nichiporuk, Andrew Radin, Olesya Tkacheva, and Jenny Oberholtzer, "Lessons from Russia's Operations in Crimea and Eastern Ukraine," Santa Monica, Calif.: RAND Corporation, RR-1498-A, 2017. This report concludes similarly that the Russian operation in eastern Ukraine was unsuccessful as originally conceived and achieved only some of its objectives, at a much higher cost than desired.

[61]   On Russia's "Compatriot Policy," see Conley et al., 2011; Oxana Shevel, "The Politics of Citizenship Policy in Post-Soviet Russia," *Post-Soviet Affairs*, Vol. 28, No. 1, 2012; and Igor Zevelev, "Russia's Policy Toward Compatriots in the Former Soviet Union," *Russia in Global Affairs*, Vol. 6, No. 1, January–March 2008.

shows. These TV stations subtly weave Putin's messages in between these programs.[62] Similarly, a report on Russian soft-power influence in Estonia notes that

> Estonians and non-Estonians live in different information spaces, often with contrasting content. . . . Most of the Russian-speaking population derives its information and views on history and current events from Russian television channels that are directly subordinate to the Kremlin and can be used as a mechanism of propaganda.[63]

A former Latvian government official observed, however, that the Russian media mixes two separate messages—one intended for internal Russian audiences, which emphasizes Putin's authority, and the other, for external audiences, which hypes the U.S. imperialist threat. The two messages sometimes are at odds with each other, undermining the overall impact of the message.[64]

In Poland, officials and researchers interviewed saw Russian attempts at eliciting pro-Russian feelings as unlikely to succeed. However, there was wide agreement that exploiting anti-Ukrainian feelings that exist in parts of the Polish population, using slogans such as "why pay for the Ukrainians and send them all this aid, when there are so many internal problems in Poland?" fell on receptive ears and undercut Polish assistance policy toward Ukraine.[65] In addition to anti-Ukrainian messaging, the Russian communication campaign in Poland stresses more pacifist themes along the lines of "we [Poles] should not respond to the Russians the same way as they act." In this sense, Russia echoes the line of argument made by the German left, among others.[66] Russia has also tried to inflame anti-Polish feelings in Kaliningrad. For

---

[62] Interview with Latvian think tank analysts, July 15, 2015.

[63] Mike Winnerstig, ed., "Tools of Destabilization: Russian Soft Power and Non-Military Influence in the Baltic States," Sweden Defense Research Agency, December 16, 2014, p. 53.

[64] Interview with former Latvian government official, July 15, 2015.

[65] Interviews with Polish officials and think tank analysts, July 2015.

[66] Interviews with Polish analysts, July 14. 2015.

instance, local media in Kaliningrad published stories about Russians being allegedly poorly treated or intimidated in Poland.[67]

Russia's strategic communication efforts have a harder time finding an audience beyond the Baltic States and Poland. Russian-televised programs in Finland promote the idea that Russians are ill treated in Finland, but the impact of these stories is limited by the fact that most of the country's 60,000-strong Russian minority speak Finnish and are well integrated in Finnish society—two factors that make them less likely to base their judgment solely on Russian media.[68]

While many Swedish officials are concerned about the spread of Russian propaganda in the Baltics and other former members of the Soviet Union and Warsaw Pact countries, there is limited concern that Russia would be able to sway Swedes to its cause. Sweden, like much of the European Union, seems to have difficulty formulating a coherent response to the Russian propaganda challenge. Swedish officials were insistent that the government not produce its own countermessage and were generally supportive of the proposal within the European Union to support independent media in the Eastern Partnership countries. There does appear to be some military-produced strategic communications, following a history of generally well-perceived military-produced propaganda in Sweden during the Cold War.[69]

One French official noted that the Russian "propaganda machine" is active in France,[70] but one researcher described Russian efforts to influence the political debate in France as "messy," "transparent," and overall not very successful. Such efforts include the creation of the Democracy and Cooperation Institute (Institut de la démocratie et de la coopération [IDC]), led by a former Russian member of parliament (MP). IDC works to improve the image of Russia but is generally seen

---

[67] Interview with Polish analyst, July 13, 2015.

[68] Interview with Finnish official, May 28, 2015.

[69] Interviews with Swedish officials and journalists, July 20 and 21, 2015.

[70] Interview with French government-affiliated think tank analyst, June 18, 2015.

as Russian propaganda.[71] A number of other pro-Russia forums might be more successful, such as the Franco-Russian Dialogue Association (Association Dialogue Franco-Russe), whose discourse is less pro-Putin than IDC, giving it more credibility.[72] In July 2015, the copresident of this association, who is also a member of the French Parliament, led a controversial trip to Moscow and Crimea with ten fellow MPs.[73] These efforts, however, are counterbalanced by very vocal Ukrainian civil-society actors present in France.[74]

Perceptions of NATO and the United States

Perceptions of NATO

European countries, particularly eastern NATO members, are concerned that the Alliance is ill equipped to respond to the current crisis with Russia and to potential further aggressions. French and Polish officials interviewed pointed out that NATO's current deterrence policy would be inadequate, in particular, if Russia were to test Article 5 "from below," i.e., with actions under the threshold of conventional war or that can be "plausibly denied" by Moscow. Such situations would make it difficult for the Alliance to reach a consensus decision—or a quick decision.[75] One Polish official mentioned the potential for divisions within NATO about how to respond to a Russian attack as a "nightmare" scenario and described the security of the Baltic States as a litmus test for NATO, since a failure to withstand Russian pressure

---

[71] Interview with French think tank analyst, June 19, 2015. See also Andrew-Sebastien Aschehoug, "Les Poupées Russes de la Propagande de Poutine en France," *Slate.fr*, February 11, 2015.

[72] Interview with French think tank analyst, June 19, 2015.

[73] Jean-Dominique Merchet, "Une Délégation de Parlementaires Français se Rend en Crimée," *L'Opinion*, July 22, 2015, updated July 27, 2015.

[74] Interview with French think tank analyst, June 19, 2015.

[75] Interview with French government-affiliated think tank analyst, June 18, 2015; interview with French government-affiliated think tank analyst, June 19, 2015; interview with Polish officials, July 14, 2015.

in the Baltics would undermine the Alliance's credibility in Poland.[76] More generally, they see Russia as trying to undermine NATO to the point where it would no longer function as a collective defense organization.[77] They claim that Russia is employing various tools for that purpose, one of which is to promote radical (and anti-NATO) parties in Europe.[78] Some media accounts and many officials have emphasized the risks of divisions within NATO based on geography or political differences. While countries closer to Russia tend to be more concerned about a threat and prefer a more assertive policy, countries farther away from Russia tend to play down the risk of future aggression and highlight concerns about an increased NATO posture provoking Russia. Senior NATO officials interviewed for this study mostly played down internal divisions. Another senior NATO official interviewed believed that Europeans would follow U.S. leadership and not object strenuously to prepositioning forces in the Baltics.[79] A third observed that there was a history of member states opting out of particular NATO decisions with which they disagreed without it undermining the overall coherence of the Alliance.[80] So far, there has been relatively little opposition within NATO to intensified U.S. military activity in the Baltics since the summer of 2015. When asked about the influence of the far right or far left, officials responded that they did not believe that parties on either extreme were strongly influencing countries' policies toward Russia or NATO.[81] Overall, NATO officials interviewed defended the idea that the Alliance is in the process of developing a stronger policy toward Russia.[82]

---

[76] Interview with Polish official, July 14, 2015.

[77] Interviews with Polish analysts, July 14, 2015.

[78] Interview with Polish officials, July 13, 2015. On Russia's support to populist parties in Europe, see Larrabee et al., 2017.

[79] Interview with NATO official, June 15, 2015.

[80] Interview with NATO official, June 16, 2015.

[81] Interviews with NATO officials, June 15, 2015.

[82] Interviews with NATO officials, June 15–17, 2015.

 There are concerns about the degree of popular support in Europe for the core principle behind NATO: collective defense. A June 2015 Pew Research Center survey of main NATO states showed that the willingness to use military force to defend a NATO ally attacked by Russia was limited, from 38 percent in Germany to 49 percent in the United Kingdom. Even in the United States and Canada, supporters of the use of force to defend a NATO ally barely reached a majority (56 percent and 53 percent, respectively).[83] This points to weak support for collective defense on the part of most NATO allies. German analysts, however, questioned the survey, and argued that German hesitation regarding collective defense drew on the experience of past missions such as Afghanistan.[84] Several of our interlocutors contended that, if Russia were to clearly demonstrate aggression against a NATO country, there would be a far stronger consensus toward collective defense.[85] Indeed, while Europeans seem wary of their commitments to NATO, the Alliance still enjoys strong popular support. A comparison of opinions[86] regarding NATO between 2013 and 2015 shows that support for NATO has increased in five of the six European countries surveyed, with the exception of Germany, where unfavorable opinions have increased (see Figure 2.4).[87] These results suggest that European opinion of NATO is somewhat decoupled from the understanding of the commitment it potentially represents, with NATO being seen more as a U.S. umbrella than as a collective defense alliance.

---

[83] Simmons, Stokes, and Poushter, 2015, p. 5.

[84] Interview with German officials, an academic, and think tank analysts, June 16–19, 2015.

[85] Interviews with German and Swedish officials and think tank analysts, June 16–19, July 21–22, 2015.

[86] Defined as the sum of "very favorable" and "somewhat favorable" opinions.

[87] For comparison, opinion toward NATO has remained stable in the United States between 2013 and 2015, with 49 percent holding combined "very favorable" and "somewhat favorable" opinions; see Simmons, Stokes, and Poushter, 2015, p. 47.

Figure 2.4
Evolution of Favorable Opinion Toward NATO Between 2013 and 2015

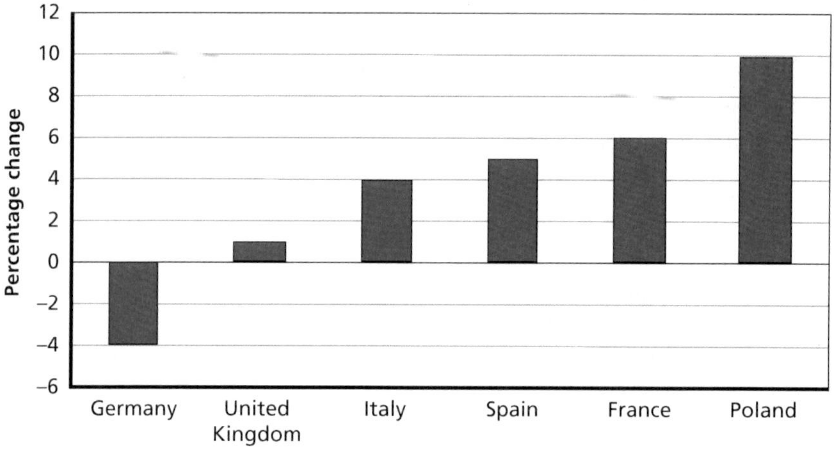

SOURCE: Data from Simmons, Stokes, and Poushter, 2015, p. 47.
RAND *RR1579-2.4*

Perceptions of the United States

The United States is still seen as a key guarantor of European security. U.S. and European officials interviewed emphasized the critical importance of U.S. leadership in NATO and recognized the importance of the U.S. military presence for maintaining security in Europe.[88] German analysts interviewed underscored the importance of the transatlantic relationship for Germany and acknowledged that the U.S. presence in Europe was essential to maintain European security.[89] Many Swedes see the United States as playing a major security role in Europe.[90] The Baltic countries recognize that, on their own, they can do little to deter Russia from taking military actions that threaten their security. They therefore have pressed for the stationing of U.S. troops on their territory. Estonian and Latvian officials interviewed see the presence of a U.S. battalion in each Baltic State (with a total of a brigade in all three

---

[88] Interviews and discussions with NATO officials, June 15, 16, 17, and 23, 2015.

[89] Interviews with German think tank analysts and academic, June 18 and 19, 2015.

[90] "B-52 Bombers to Exercise over Sweden," Radio Sweden, May 20, 2015.

countries) as necessary to deter a Russian attack and recognize that the United States is the most reliable source of political and military support. They see other NATO forces deployed in the Baltics as an additional asset designed to strengthen their security. At the same time, they believe that only the presence of U.S. forces on their soil can effectively deter Russia. As a result, they have given priority to strengthening their relationship with the United States over interactions with the rest of the NATO countries.[91] Polish officials interviewed stressed that the credibility of Article 5 ultimately depends on U.S. actions and policy,[92] and they see Russia as trying to weaken Western security structures (European Union and NATO) and separate the United States from its European allies.[93]

The United States is generally viewed positively in Europe. A median of 68 percent of respondents in key NATO member states surveyed in June 2015[94] believed the United States would use military force to defend a NATO ally, were that NATO ally to find itself in a serious military conflict with Russia. Poland represents an important exception, with only 49 percent of those surveyed believing the United States would do so.[95]

Yet, the appreciation for the U.S. role in Europe does not come without reservations. In Sweden, generally positive perceptions of the United States are complicated by a strong pacifist tradition, and part of the Swedish left continues to view the United States as an imperialist power.[96] On the whole, however, there is strong support for increased defense cooperation with the United States, including the purchase of U.S. arms. The more aggressive policy pursued by Russia in the Baltic

---

[91] Interviews with Estonian and Latvian officials, July 15 and 17, 2015.

[92] Interview with Polish officials, July 13, 2015.

[93] Interview with Polish official, July 13, 2015.

[94] Canada, France, Germany, Italy, Poland, Spain, the United Kingdom, and the United States.

[95] Simmons, Stokes, and Poushter, 2015, p. 54.

[96] Left-wing parties, for example, expressed negative opinions about American B-52s that participated in a recent exercise in Sweden. See "B-52 Bombers to Exercise Over Sweden," 2015.

region and High North has increased Swedish interest in strengthening defense cooperation with NATO, as underscored by the Host Nation Support Agreements signed by Sweden at the NATO summit in Wales in September 2014. In Germany, while there has been a marked shift in German attitudes toward Russia, with support for Russia declining visibly since the illegal annexation of Crimea and the downing of Malaysian Airlines Flight 17 over Ukraine in July 2014,[97] there is still a small but vocal group of anti-American individuals.[98] They question whether the United States respects the fundamental rights critical to Germany's self-image, particularly after the revelations that the U.S. National Security Agency had been tapping the communications of key German political leaders, including Chancellor Merkel. Germany shows fewer opinions favorable to the United States than France, the United Kingdom, or Spain, for instance (only 50 percent have favorable opinions, compared with 73 percent, 66 percent, and 65 percent, respectively, in the three other countries).[99] One interviewee, however, emphasized that polling revealed that there was not necessarily a correlation between anti-American and pro-Russian views.[100]

In France, both anti-American and pro-Russian currents still exist in certain parts of French society, are present within the parliament, and have relays in the media.[101] As indicated earlier, however, the anti-American sentiment remains limited, with three-quarters of the French holding a favorable opinion of the United States, according to a 2015 poll by the Pew Research Center.[102] Russia generally has a positive image in French public opinion: A January 2015 poll showed that 81 percent "fully agreed" or "somewhat agreed" with the statement that

---

[97]   On the evolution of public opinion toward Russia in Germany and France, see Larrabee et al., 2017.

[98]   Interview with German academic, June 19, 2015.

[99]   Richard Wike, Bruce Stokes, and Jacob Poushter, "Global Public Back U.S. on Fighting ISIS, But Are Critical of Post-9/11 Torture," comment on Pew Research Center Spring 2015 *Global Attitudes Survey*, June 23, 2015, Question 12a.

[100]   Interviews with German official and an academic, June 19, 2015.

[101]   Interview with French think tank analyst, June 19, 2015.

[102]   Wike, Stokes, and Poushter, 2015, Question 12a.

"Russia is a great country with whom France should maintain good relations."[103] A French official, however, noted that this image bears little connection with what is happening in Russia and is more of a reaction to the feeling that the United States is imposing a policy.[104] Some have expressed a concern that the United States may be tempted to escalate tension with Russia, possibly under the pressure of eastern NATO members.[105] French Director of Military Intelligence General Christophe Gomart stated in April 2015 testimony before the Defense Committee of the French National Assembly that NATO's intelligence mistakenly announced that Russia would massively invade Ukraine, while his agency did not believe this would be the case, and blamed the "predominance of U.S. intelligence in NATO's intelligence" as the reason why this assessment was so alarmist.[106]

---

[103] Damien Philippot and Esteban Pratviel, "Les Français, la Perception du Conflit Ukraino-Russe et la Livraison de Navires de Guerre à la Russie," poll of the Institut Français d'Opinion Publique for *La Tribune*, January 2015, p. 6.

[104] Interview with French government-affiliated think tank analyst, June 18, 2015.

[105] Interview with French officials, May 12, 2015.

[106] Assemblée Nationale hearing of General Christophe Gomart, Commission de la Défense Nationale et des Forces Armées, Briefing No. 49, March 25, 2015. See also Jean-Dominique Merchet, "Ukraine: les Français ont une vision 'plus mitigée' que l'Otan," Blog Secret Défense, *L'Opinion*, August 29, 2014.

CHAPTER THREE

Responses

In response to the Ukrainian crisis, European countries have adopted a broad range of measures that include economic sanctions, support to the Ukrainian government, enhanced military preparedness, reassurance measures for eastern NATO members, adaptation of the Alliance to the new security environment, increased cooperation with European non-NATO members, and measures to counter Russia's information campaign in Europe. These measures seek to not only sanction Russia for its behavior in Ukraine, but also deter it from undertaking any further aggressive moves. For many countries, however, this response has also included keeping channels of communication open with Moscow on a number of issues, from the implementation of the Minsk II agreement to counterterrorism.

European States Agree on a Firm Response to Russia

That Russia's behavior requires a strong response is widely accepted by most European countries. Even in Germany—a country sometimes accused of having excessive sympathies for Russia[1]—there is strong support within the ruling coalition and elite opinion for Chancellor

---

[1]   See, for instance, Rick Noack, "Why Do Nearly 40 Percent of Germans Endorse Russia's Annexation of Crimea?" *Washington Post*, November 28, 2014; Ralf Neukirch, "Is Germany a Country of Russia Apologists?" *Spiegel*, March 31, 2014; "Germany and Russia: How Very Understanding," *Economist*, May 10, 2014; and Stephen Evans, "Germans Not Keen to Ruffle Russian Feathers," *BBC News* magazine, April 12, 2014.

Merkel's basic position that Russia has violated commitments undertaken after the end of the Cold War and that its actions in Ukraine threaten European security. There is also an understanding that the West needs to strengthen its defense posture to be able to deter further aggressive moves on the part of Russia.[2]

Demonstrating the Cost of Russian Aggression: Economic Sanctions
The 28 EU member states have achieved and maintained a consensus on sanctions since the beginning of the crisis.[3] Norway, although not part of the EU, supports the EU line and implements similar sanctions.[4] Sanctions have included, as early as March 2014, assets freeze and travel bans for specific individuals linked to Russia's actions in Ukraine and, since July 2014, targeted economic sanctions against Russia.[5] On March 19, 2015, President of the European Council Donald Tusk announced that "the duration of economic sanctions will be clearly linked to the complete implementation of the Minsk agreements."[6] One EU official knowledgeable about EU sanctions pointed out how unusual that statement was, as the EU generally keeps criteria for termination much vaguer.[7] The EU package of targeted economic sanctions was designed to have the maximum impact on the Russian economy while also having the lowest impact on the European Union and spreading—when possible—the pain across member

---

[2]   Angela Merkel, Speech by Federal Chancellor on the Occasion of the 51st Munich Security Conference, Munich, February 7, 2015; "Merkel Toughens Up," *Economist*, November 19, 2014; interviews with German think tank analysts and an academic, June 18 and 19, 2015.

[3]   Interview with EU official, June 3, 2015.

[4]   Interview with Norwegian officials, July 14, 2015.

[5]   For a detailed time line of the European Union's restrictive measures against Russia, see "Timeline—EU Restrictive Measures in Response to the Crisis in Ukraine," Brussels, European Council, undated.

[6]   "Remarks by President Donald Tusk After the First Session of the European Council Meeting," Brussels, European Council, March 19, 2015.

[7]   Interview with EU official, June 16, 2015.

states.[8] The EU Commission mitigates this impact to some extent by providing subsidies to those member states most affected.[9] In spite of increasing divisions within the European Union on whether sanctions are justified—with Italy and Hungary increasingly reluctant to follow other EU members on this policy—they were prolonged again in December 2016 and March 2017 as some important elements of the peace process were seen as not yet fulfilled.[10]

Several French and Polish interviewees noted that European solidarity on sanctions—and on their successive renewals—was a big surprise for Putin.[11] Yet, maintaining a consensus is challenging because of the different relations each EU member has with Russia.[12] Polish discussants found it "remarkable" that Western sanctions on Russia have lasted this long, particularly in view of the fissures that already exist within the European Union, citing pro-Russian inclinations on the part of Slovakia, Hungary, and Greece.[13] Italy, too, has expressed strong reservations toward the continuation of economic sanctions against Russia.[14] According to one French researcher, Moscow is betting on the fact that the EU project is going to explode, as Putin does not believe it will be able to hold in the long term.[15] This analysis was shared by an EU official who noted that Russia uses the differences

---

[8]   Interview with EU official, June 16, 2015.

[9]   Interview with EU official, June 16, 2015. This is done through the Common Agricultural Policy—no special fund was created for this purpose. The European Union does not compensate member states with indirect costs, however—for instance, the United Kingdom's losses in terms of financial services (interview with EU official, June 16, 2015).

[10]   James Kanter, "E.U. to Extend Sanctions Against Russia, but Divisions Show," *New York Times*, December 18, 2015; Robin Emmott and Gabriela Baczynska, "Italy, Hungary Say No Automatic Renewal of Russia Sanctions," Reuters, March 14, 2016.

[11]   Interview with French officials, June 18, 2015; interview with French think tank analyst, June 19, 2015; interview with Polish official, July 14, 2015.

[12]   Interview with French officials, June 18, 2015; interview with French government–affiliated think tank analyst, June 19, 2015.

[13]   Interview with Polish analysts, July 14, 2015.

[14]   Kanter, 2015.

[15]   Interview with French think tank analyst, June 18, 2015.

of views that exist between various EU countries to attempt to divide them.[16] Although these attempts have so far been unsuccessful, as evidenced by the renewed consensus of the 28 on sanctions, they represent additional tensions for the European Union at a time when it is already struggling with other centrifugal forces from the migrants crisis to the "Brexit" vote.

Supporting Ukraine and the Minsk Process

Another EU priority—and another area of consensus—is to support the full implementation of the Minsk II agreement and to help Ukraine reform. As one EU official noted, "Helping Ukraine get internally strong is the best thing we can do."[17] To this end, the European Union provides political, economic, and financial aid.[18] This also comes with a widespread understanding that helping Ukraine is going to be challenging, because of this country's abysmal record with regard to development, governance, and transparency. As one EU official put it: "historically, Ukraine never delivered when it promised reforms, but it is now expected to do so while it is fighting a war."[19] Support to Ukraine is seen as a long-term endeavor that is also the only way that Ukraine can avoid going through a second or third "Maidan" revolution in the future.[20]

In addition to EU financial support, Ukraine's signature of the Deep and Comprehensive Free Trade Area (DCFTA), part of the Association Agreement with the European Union, will represent additional revenue for Ukraine and help finance reform in the country.[21] Another

---

[16]   Interview with EU official, June 3, 2015.

[17]   Interview with EU official, June 16, 2015.

[18]   Interview with EU official, June 16, 2015. EU financial support to Ukraine was 1.6 billion euros in 2014. In January 2015, the European Commission issued a proposal for increasing this amount to 1.8 billion euros in 2015 in the form of a Macro-Financial Assistance—MFA—program (interview with EU official, June 10, 2015; "Ukraine/Macro-Financial Assistance," Brussels, European Commission, updated July 22, 2015.)

[19]   Interview with EU official, June 17, 2015.

[20]   Interview with EU official, June 17, 2015.

[21]   Interview with EU official, June 10, 2015.

key measure adopted by the European Council was to establish in July 2014 an EU Advisory Mission for Civilian Security Sector Reform Ukraine that works at the strategic level in Kyiv to provide "strategic advice for the development of effective, sustainable and accountable security services that contribute to strengthening the rule of law in Ukraine."[22] Finally, the European Union supports the Special Monitoring Mission of the Organization for Security and Cooperation in Europe (OSCE) to Ukraine. The European Union provides the mission with funds, equipment such as armored vehicles, planning capacity, and satellite imagery from the EU Satellite Center in Torrejón (Spain).[23]

NATO has also provided assistance to strengthen the Ukrainian government, including through trust funds for logistics and command, control, communications, computers, and intelligence.[24] NATO international staff highlighted frustration with bureaucratic resistance to reform within the Ukrainian government. Some officials were also skeptical that the new government would be significantly more eager to pursue major structuring of the Ukrainian security establishment than previous governments.[25]

Individual European countries also provide support. Examples include Germany placing a strong emphasis on bolstering the impact of the OSCE during its chairmanship of the organization.[26] It has also worked at strengthening the Ukrainian government though bi- and multilateral assistance. German officials believe that helping Ukraine to have a stronger and more effective state will both further European

---

[22] Former EU High Representative for Foreign Affairs and Security Policy Catherine Ashton, as quoted in EEAS, "EUAM Ukraine," EEAS web page, undated(a).

[23] Interview with EU official, June 15, 2015; interview with EU official, June 17, 2015.

[24] See "NATO's Practical Support to Ukraine," fact sheet, North Atlantic Treaty Organization, June 2015.

[25] Interviews with NATO officials and discussions with Ukrainian officials, April–June 2015.

[26] Interviews with German think tank analysts, discussions at conference, June 18 and 22, 2015.

integration and counter Putin's agenda.[27] Norway has increased its support in Ukraine, particularly on energy and governance issues.[28] Estonia and Latvia appear aligned with the rest of the European Union on their Ukraine policy, including limiting support sent to Ukraine to nonlethal materiel. Estonian officials noted that they are planning to send their special forces to train their counterparts in Ukraine.[29] These countries are well aware of the impact that a political and economic collapse of Ukraine might have on the region. Poland, in particular, fears an implosion of the Ukrainian state that would send waves of instability (in the form of refugees, weapons, or criminal networks) to its territory.[30]

Although there is an extensive list of support measures, it is not yet clear that European and NATO efforts have had a sustainable impact on reform in Ukraine. While our interviews certainly highlighted the ongoing political challenges of reform in Ukraine, Ukrainian officials emphasized their frustration with the slow pace and complex NATO bureaucracy in Brussels. In some cases, Ukrainian officials and NATO officials accused one another of being the source of delay for assistance programs.[31] Some Ukrainian officials were also frustrated that the Europeans did not more strongly condemn Russian aggression and offer direct support of Ukrainian operations in eastern Ukraine.[32] The ongoing migration crisis and war in Syria reduce the likelihood that a strong European assistance to Ukraine will persist.

Improving Military Preparedness and Responding to Future Threats

Countries that feel most threatened by Russia militarily have worked on improving their preparedness, although, given the small size of

---

[27] Interviews with German think tank analysts, discussions at conference, June 18 and 22, 2015.

[28] Interview with Norwegian officials, July 14, 2015.

[29] Interviews with Estonian and Latvian officials, July 15 and 17, 2015.

[30] Interview with Polish analyst, July 13, 2015.

[31] Interviews with NATO officials and discussions with Ukrainian officials, April–June 2015.

[32] Interviews with Ukrainian officials, April–August 2015.

these countries, the size of their forces remains limited. This is especially applicable to the Baltic States; while all of them understand they cannot stop a conventional Russian invasion on their own, their efforts aim at imposing maximum costs on any such invading forces and delaying their advance. The thick forests in some parts of these countries favor the defense by channeling avenues of approach, and the Baltic States have paid great attention to preparing the terrain for defense. Estonia's Hedgehog exercise in May 2015 involved 13,000 Estonian personnel—a substantial number, given the country's population size of 1.3 million.[33] Latvia, despite its larger population, has an active ground force of only 3,900, compared with Estonia's 5,500, and a volunteer National Guard comparable to the Kaitscliit (the Estonian Defense League organization akin to the U.S. National Guard) of approximately 8,000.[34] Western observers were generally more critical of the leadership, preparedness, and coordination of the Latvian security forces.[35] One Latvian professor noted that his country's level of attention to preparedness against Russia has risen greatly in recent years.[36]

In April 2015, the Finnish Coast Guard dropped depth charges on a possible Russian submarine in Finnish waters to show that such an incursion was crossing a red line.[37] The government also sent a letter

---

[33] Interview with foreign official based in Tallinn, July 16, 2015; Ben Farmer and David Blair, "Estonia Stages Biggest Military Exercise in Country's History Amid Fears of Russian 'Aggression,'" *Telegraph*, May 12, 2015. Estonians explain their strong response to Russia by their history in World War II. They note that the country did not strongly oppose the Soviet takeover and spent 45 years under occupation. The lesson from this mistake is to fiercely oppose any Russian attack (interview with Estonian academic, July 17, 2015).

[34] "Latvia," *Jane's World's Armies*, July 2015; NATO, "NATO Publishes Defence Expenditures Data for 2014 and Estimates for 2015: Financial and Economic Data Relating to NATO Defence," press release PR/CP(2015) 093-COR1, June 22, 2015.

[35] Interview with foreign contractor working in Latvia and NATO country officials, July 15 and 16, 2015.

[36] Interview with Latvian academic, July 15, 2015.

[37] Interview with Finnish official, May 28, 2015. See also Sam LaGrone, "Finns Drop Depth Charges Against 'Possible Underwater Object' near Helsinki," *U.S. Naval Institute News*, April 28, 2015.

to the country's 900,000 reservists during the summer of 2015 to clarify their status with regard to the reserves and let them know what would happen if they had to mobilize; this was an expected step in the implementation of the reform of the reserves carried out in 2011 but also, in the context of the tensions with Russia, a signal that the system is working and that the Finnish government is ready to activate it if needed. Finland continues to carry out its usual large exercises for conscripts, including one in June 2015 that took place near the border with Russia in which 10,000 Finns participated.[38] Sweden is also boosting its defense capacity, including through the acquisition of short-, medium-, and long-range air defenses.[39]

NATO Adaptation and Reassurance Measures

At the September 2014 Wales summit, NATO considered two possible options for responding to the Russian threat and providing deterrence and assurance. One was establishing a forward presence in the Baltics. The other was having the ability to rapidly deploy forces. Some NATO countries, including Germany, highlighted two major risks of the first option: A forward presence might not only provoke Russia but would also be contrary to the 1997 NATO-Russia Founding Act, which limited the "permanent stationing of substantial combat forces" on the territory of NATO's eastern members.[40] Interviewees in Poland and the Baltic States were of the opposite view that forward presence would deter rather than provoke Russia—particularly as Putin was deemed to respect only strength—and that Russia's illegal annexation of Crimea and the attempt to destabilize eastern Ukraine had violated the NATO-Russia Founding Act and rendered it obsolete.[41]

---

[38] This exercise came just after the NATO multinational exercise that mobilized 14,000 people in Estonia (interview with Finnish official, July 14, 2015).

[39] Interview with Swedish officials, July and October 2015.

[40] NATO, "Founding Act on Mutual Relations, Cooperation and Security Between NATO and the Russian Federation," May 1997.

[41] Interviews with NATO officials, June 15 and 16, 2015; interviews with Estonian, Latvian, and Polish officials, July 13, 15, and 17, 2015.

At the Wales Summit, the Alliance chose the second option and decided to enhance its capacity to rapidly deploy forces in a crisis through the Readiness Action Plan (RAP). One official noted that Poland and the Baltic countries' acceptance of the RAP reflected a pragmatic assessment that, even though NATO would not deploy forward troops, it would likely continue to receive significant bilateral assistance, including a rotational presence, from the United States. Several NATO officials emphasized that the RAP should be seen as a first point, or the floor, in NATO's adaptation, rather than an early reaction that NATO would reverse. Other measures that could receive increased support from allies might include larger exercises, a nuclear deterrence component, or a move toward a greater rotational or forward presence on the eastern flank.[42] The RAP is not specifically targeted at Russia and explicitly seeks to respond to the threat by ISIL and Islamic extremism in the south.

Following the Wales Summit, NATO took several steps toward implementing the RAP. The first and most concrete is the establishment of the Very High Readiness Joint Task Force (VJTF), a brigade-size force capable of deploying in seven days, with leadership rotating among seven framework nations.[43] Second, NATO and Supreme Headquarters Allied Powers Europe (SHAPE) are working to speed

---

[42] One official at SHAPE explained that the elements of the RAP had already been discussed prior to the beginning of the Ukraine crisis, and this plan was put into place quickly once the crisis occurred as a stopgap measure. He explained that NATO was discussing ways to strengthen its policy towards Russia. Interviews with NATO officials, June 15–17, 2015.

[43] A NATO Parliamentary Assembly report explains:

> The VJTF forces, up to 5,000 strong (brigade-level), will be supplied in rotation from Allies. One Ally, in an annual rotation, will act as the framework nation for the force, though two to three nations might be needed to support the maintenance of the brigade's scale-up and scale-down readiness. . . . The VJTF is a multinational brigade with up to five manoeuvre battalions with standing headquarters. As a whole, the brigade will be deployable within seven days at most in its full capability, which includes air and maritime support, and chemical, biological, radiological, and nuclear defence capabilities. At a minimum, at least one battalion of the brigade should be deployable within 48 hours (NATO Defence and Security Committee, "The Readiness Action Plan: Assurance and Deterrence for the Post-2014 Security Environment," NATO Parliamentary Assembly, April 16, 2015).

decisionmaking within the North Atlantic Council, including through tabletop exercises. Third, NATO is improving its processes for sharing intelligence assessments to make it easier for the Alliance to make a decision more rapidly in the case of an ambiguous threat in the Baltics. To date, intelligence sharing in NATO has been relatively limited and tends to be more based on case-by-case exchange of information rather than full collaboration. Fourth, NATO is working to improve logistics and infrastructure for movement across Europe. Fifth, NATO has discussed giving more authority to Supreme Allied Commander Europe (SACEUR) and other commanders. While SACEUR has the authority to stage and alert the NATO Response Force (NRF), discussions about enabling SACEUR to deploy forces have stalled, as national political authorities are reluctant to entrust this authority to NATO commanders.[44]

Finally, NATO developed a "comprehensive hybrid strategy" containing three elements: *prepare*, which includes developing indicators and warnings to provide knowledge and attribution of Russia's actions; *deter*, which includes identifying economic and military actions to make aggression costly to Russia; and *defend*, which involves strategic communication, cybersecurity, and other measures to protect NATO members from Russian aggression.[45] One NATO defense planner explained that, while the country under attack had to be the first responder, NATO or its member states would be prepared to quickly offer support. He also noted that, while consensus was the "cornerstone" of NATO decisionmaking, individual allies could certainly provide assistance without consensus.[46] Another NATO official highlighted the significant capability of Russian special operations forces, observing that they were putting in practice the same "playbook" as U.S. special operations forces had used in the past for developing or supporting insurgencies.[47] Hence, while NATO governments have

---

[44] Interviews with NATO officials, June 15 and 16, 2015.

[45] Interview with NATO official, June 16, 2015.

[46] Interview with NATO official, June 16, 2015.

[47] Interviews with NATO officials, June 17, 2015.

agreed on a relatively measured policy with respect to Russia, planners at NATO headquarters and SHAPE perceive Russia as posing a significant and complex threat and are working to develop options to address it.

Following the Wales Summit, there were significant question whether NATO's adaptation was sufficient.[48] A range of interlocutors seemed skeptical that the VJTF would provide significant numbers of deployable, high-readiness forces that would be sufficient to deter Russian aggression. Some NATO country analysts also questioned NATO's rhetoric, noting that many of NATO's terms seemed for internal political purposes and were not well understood outside of the Alliance. For example, the need to emphasize the "Very High" readiness of the VJTF name seemed to point out the limited confidence in the force. Further, the practical meaning of terms such as the Alliance's "adaptation" and improved domestic "resilience" were often unclear outside of NATO's bureaucracy.[49]

Some Polish officials interviewed noted that NATO has too little capability for high-intensity conflict and needs to improve on tanks, artillery, other heavy equipment, and infrastructure, including airports for reception of reinforcements.[50] They mentioned a need for a fully functioning brigade headquarters in Poland, with a battalion forward deployed in Poland, and with equipment sets sufficient to equip the rest of the brigade. This way, in case of a crisis, personnel could be flown in and would use the prepositioned equipment, limiting the time to readiness to a matter of days.[51] Polish officials interviewed also argued that Poland needs missile defense, especially Patriot 3, as well as helicopters for increased mobility of its forces.[52]

---

[48]   Interview with Polish officials, July 13, 2015.

[49]   Discussions with U.S. and UK think tank analysts, February 2016.

[50]   Interview with Polish officials, July 13, 2015.

[51]   Interview with Polish officials, July 13, 2015; interview with Polish officials, July 14, 2015.

[52]   Interview with Polish officials, July 14, 2015.

Polish officials interviewed acknowledged limitations in NATO's ability to respond to hybrid warfare and actions that are under the threshold of clear aggression.[53] This makes conventional deterrence all the more critical, and some called for a NATO doctrine on preemptive deployment of a spearhead force that could be activated in an area of growing danger. They argued for a permanent presence of a NATO force, arguing that a rotational presence, while useful, was inefficient as a deterrent because rotations can end at any time.[54] In addition to the permanent stationing of NATO forces in the Baltic States and Poland, they also advocated for a high-readiness NRF and additional follow-on forces behind the NRF. Finally, beside the capabilities needed, Polish officials see a need to ensure that the decisionmaking apparatus of NATO can deal adequately with such contingencies.[55] Another measure against hybrid warfare that was advocated was a step-up in intelligence cooperation.[56]

For Polish officials interviewed, the United States remains the key security provider in NATO—its presence "counts far more" than shows of solidarity from other allies[57]—and the decreased involvement of U.S. forces on the continent over the past decade is of concern to them. They noted that the actual U.S. presence in Europe has shrunk to very low levels, and there have been no exercises with U.S. heavy forces in Europe for ten years, while the changes in security environment require instead a stronger U.S. military presence.[58] Decisively keeping U.S. presence in Europe was deemed essential by officials interviewed, despite the opposition of some European members of NATO (particu-

---

[53] Interview with Polish officials, July 13, 2015; interview with Polish officials, July 14, 2015.

[54] Interview with Polish officials, July 13, 2015; interview with Polish officials, July 14, 2015.

[55] Interview with Polish official, July 13, 2015.

[56] Interview with Polish official, July 13, 2015.

[57] Interview with Polish official, July 13, 2015.

[58] Interview with Polish official, July 13, 2015.

larly Germany).[59] The United States commands a uniquely high level of confidence; if the United States were to station forces in Poland, Polish officials feel other allies would follow. Polish officials believe that U.S. troop presence would act as a "trip wire" to deter potential Russian actions, arguing that their concerns parallel those of West Germany during the Cold War.[60] Some Polish officials interviewed contend that a brigade in Poland (and Romania) and a battalion in each of the Baltic States would be sufficient as a deterrent. They acknowledge the inherent risk in such deployments but argued that it was still better than the alternative—leaving the Baltic States in a state of vulnerability.[61]

Likewise, our interlocutors in Estonia and Latvia advocated for a larger, more permanent U.S. military presence as the key response to Russian aggression. Estonian officials explained that, according to their war games and estimates of Russian special operations forces, a U.S. or NATO battalion in addition to the Estonian battalion would slow the Russian invasion sufficiently to permit Estonian forces to mobilize.[62] Latvian officials seek either a U.S. brigade across the three Baltic countries, under U.S. European Command, or a U.S. battalion "integrated into their force structure"—meaning effectively under Latvian command. Latvian officials emphasized the need for units that could act independently and be of military value in the event of a Russian invasion. They also stressed the need for U.S. forces, arguing that only the presence of U.S. forces could deter Russia, although they did emphasize that they would welcome other NATO forces, organized into a framework battalion, in addition to U.S. forces.[63] Latvian officials interviewed downplayed Russia's potential reaction to U.S. deployments as limited and expensive—at most, Russia can militarize Kaliningrad by deploying Iskander or tactical nuclear weapons there,

---

[59] Interview with Polish officials, July 14, 2015.

[60] Interview with Polish analysts, July 14, 2015.

[61] Interview with Polish officials, July 14, 2015. Our interlocutors also mentioned specific Polish military needs, to include information systems, antimissile defenses, air defense, and helicopters to improve mobility of Poland's land forces.

[62] Interviews with Estonian officials, July 17, 2015.

[63] Interview with Latvian officials, July 17, 2015.

but, according to Latvian officials, this would not significantly increase the vulnerability of the Baltic countries.[64]

In addition, both countries have numerous requests for further assistance. In Estonia, officials are interested in further developing the airfield at Amari and placing increased Estonian or U.S. air assets there; an increased naval presence, which they argue has been neglected to date; and air defense. Estonian officials emphasized that the United States should deploy sufficient capabilities to prevent Russia from being able to restrict access to the Baltics.[65] In Latvia, officials seek greater firepower for the ground forces, including Stinger missiles and artillery; better air surveillance, especially short-range and low-level radars; and armored vehicles for better ground mobility.[66]

While not permanently deployed, European NATO members have sent forces to the region that have engaged in reassurance measures such as participation in exercises, training missions, and contributions to air policing over the Baltic States. For instance, Germany and Denmark have had a lengthy presence in Poland through its participation in NATO's Northeastern Corps in Szczecin.[67] France also deployed a small armored unit (15 Leclerc tanks) for six weeks in Poland.[68] While France has been a strong supporter of implementing reassurance measures for the Baltic States, it has moderated these measures to some extent. Since January 2015, however, the number of exercises and sorties for French forces has been decreasing, due to severe budgetary constraints.[69] French forces are overstretched with Operations Barkhane (Sahel), Chammal (Iraq and Syria), and Sentinelle (defense of the homeland following the January and November

---

[64] Interview with Estonian and Latvian officials, July 15 and 17, 2015.

[65] Interview with Estonian officials, July 17, 2015.

[66] Interview with Latvian officials, July 15, 2015.

[67] Interview with Polish official, July 13, 2015.

[68] Interview with French government-affiliated think tank analyst, June 19, 2015; interview with French officials, May 12, 2015. See, also, "Déploiement d'un Détachement de Chars Leclerc à Drawsko," French Embassy in Warsaw, updated May 8, 2015.

[69] Interview with French government-affiliated think tank analyst, June 19, 2015.

2015 terrorist attacks in Paris).[70] These numerous commitments reduce France's margin of maneuver militarily and financially. As one French analyst put it, France did not commit as much attention to the crisis with Russia as it should have because there is not much it can do.[71] Another researcher noted that Russia is well aware of France's "strategic saturation" and its difficulty in establishing priorities.[72] France has also consistently advocated a diplomatic rather than military response to the crisis.[73]

The July 2016 Warsaw Summit addressed some of the concerns of the member states, especially through the announcement of an "enhanced forward presence"[74] of four multinational battalions to Poland and each of the three Baltic countries. The battalions are to be led by four framework nations—Canada, Germany, the United Kingdom, and the United States. While the battalions will rotate, so as not to become a "permanent" presence, they will effectively constitute a continuous presence. In addition, NATO announced measures to strengthen the Alliance in a range of areas, including a new hybrid strategy; improved intelligence sharing; cyber defense; and shared intelligence, surveillance, and reconnaissance capabilities. The Communiqué at Warsaw also reiterated the need for NATO to provide a strong nuclear deterrent.[75] It remains to be seen how far these improvements will address the demands of the member states. While the discussions at Warsaw did indicate the willingness of the Alliance to strengthen its response against Russia, it did not fulfill all expectations in this regard.

---

[70] Interview with French officials, June 18, 2015; interview with French government-affiliated think tank analyst, June 18, 2015.

[71] Interview with French government-affiliated think tank analyst, June 19, 2015.

[72] Interview with French think tank analyst, June 18, 2015.

[73] Interview with French think tank analyst, June 19, 2015; Merchet, 2014.

[74] NATO, *Warsaw Summit Communiqué*, July 9, 2016, para. 40.

[75] NATO, 2016.

Increased Cooperation of Non-NATO Countries

European countries that are not members of NATO have taken measures that underscore their commitment to the security of the Alliance's eastern flank. Although it has no legally binding commitment to defend the Baltic States should Russia pose a threat to their independence and security, Sweden made a solidarity declaration in 2009 that states its intention to defend other EU members (although this has not been reciprocated). Swedish officials and analysts emphasize that Sweden would likely view Russian military actions in the Baltics as provocative.[76] Swedish military officials recognize that access to Swedish bases and other facilities would be strategically important, especially for the U.S Air Force, in the event of a Russian attack on the Baltic States. They understand that the U.S. Air Force would want to be sufficiently close to the Baltic countries to provide airborne refueling and early warning, which makes basing in current U.S. bases in Germany suboptimal, while stationing military aircraft in Poland or the Baltic States would make them vulnerable to Russian attack.[77]

Sweden is constrained from making any firm military commitment to defend the Baltic States by its longstanding policy of neutrality or "non-alignment," as it is officially termed since Sweden's accession to the European Union,[78] yet it has taken a variety of measures to build increasingly close security ties to countries in the region.[79] Sweden and Finland conduct regular exercises and joint military planning, and even make use of each other's air bases. Through NORDEFCO, Sweden

---

[76]   Interviews with Swedish officials, July 21, 2015.

[77]   Interview with Swedish think tank analyst, July 21, 2015.

[78]   The "non-alignment" policy remains popular with the electorate, especially the Social Democrats. Observers of Swedish politics noted widespread Swedish concerns about Russian aggression and highlighted feelings of solidarity with the Baltic States among the center-right parties. They did warn that there could be strong opposition from the left and far right if Sweden took sides in a Russian attack, since such an action would undermine Swedish neutrality (interviews with Swedish journalists, July 20 and 21, 2015). A telling example of the extent and limits of Swedish policy is that, while Sweden does not participate in exercises explicitly for Article 5 defense of NATO member states, it participates in similar activities under a different name (interviews with Swedish officials, July 21, 2015).

[79]   Matt Ford, "After Crimea, Sweden Flirts with Joining NATO," *Atlantic*, March 12, 2014.

has also intensified defense cooperation with Norway, Denmark, and Iceland. Sweden participated in large NATO exercises, such as Arctic Challenge,[80] and Swedish officials repeatedly affirmed their interest in engaging in joint exercises in the Baltics with U.S. and other NATO forces in the future. While there were specific training goals for these exercises, Sweden seems especially interested in building closer ties that could enhance its ability to provide assistance to the Baltic States in the event of a crisis.[81] Government officials stated that they sought to build partnership and cooperation just short of membership.[82] Sweden is one of five NATO countries pursuing an "Enhanced Opportunities Partners Program" with NATO.[83] Closer defense cooperation with NATO, especially the ability to host NATO forces, was discussed at the Wales Summit, and Finland already has adopted some of the necessary changes in its laws that would enable such enhanced defense cooperation to take place. For its part, Sweden is reexamining the technical legal framework surrounding hosting NATO forces.[84] Finland is also examining its legislation to see what changes need to be made to enhance cooperation with Sweden.[85]

Countering Russian Propaganda and the Cyber Threat

NATO officials interviewed recognized Russia's ability to use strategic communication tools to internally destabilize some of its neighbors, as well as NATO's lack of tools to address this issue. In general, they believed that NATO headquarters and other Alliance institutions would be ineffective or unable to respond because of their limited capa-

---

[80] Jonathan Wade, "Norway-Led Arctic Challenge Exercise 2015 Starts," Sentinel Analytical Group, May 25, 2015.

[81] Interviews with Swedish officials, July 20–21, 2015.

[82] Interviews with Swedish officials, July 21, 2015.

[83] NATO, *Wales Summit Declaration*, September 5, 2014, para. 88.

[84] Interviews with Swedish officials, July 21, 2015.

[85] Interview with Finnish official, July 14, 2015. Finland's law currently authorizes joint training and exercises, as well as participation in international crisis management operations (under UN, EU, and NATO auspices), but it is unclear what Finland could do if its neighbor required direct military assistance following a Russian aggression.

bilities in the area of strategic communication.[86] This is believed to give Russia a significant advantage, despite recent progress in establishing the NATO Centre of Excellence for Strategic Communication in Riga, for example, to share best practices among member governments.[87] While improved strategic communications is clearly a priority, it does not seem to have gotten off the ground.[88]

Similar difficulties exist at the national level. One French official noted that France has little means to respond to Russian strategic communication efforts.[89] One researcher pointed to a lack of expertise on Russia in France: "We forgot to follow what was going on in Russia."[90] The German Ministry of Foreign Affairs started taking steps to address the "expertise gap" by funding a new research institute specializing in Russia and Eurasia.[91] Germany also supports Russian-language broadcasting in the Baltics.[92] At the EU level, there is awareness that instrumentalization by Russia of Russophone minorities in some member states might be problematic. One EU official mentioned that the topic of the rights of Russian-speaking minority populations is very difficult and sensitive, given that Estonia and Latvia are EU member states. Similarly, there is awareness that Russia is financing some political parties in Europe,[93] but these are matters of internal politics and regulations that are outside the EU scope of action.

---

[86] Interviews and discussions with NATO officials, June 15, 16, 17, and 23, 2015. Officials mentioned a similar inability to counter ISIL's communication strategy.

[87] Interviews and discussions with NATO officials, June 15, 16, 17, and 23, 2015.

[88] Interview with foreign contractors working in Latvia, July 15, 2015.

[89] Interview with French officials, June 18, 2015.

[90] Interview with French think tank analyst, June 19, 2015. One individual interviewed offered a different view, noting that France was "rearming" intellectually on Russia, developing and refining analyses about Russia (interview with French government-affiliated think tank analyst, June 19, 2015).

[91] Interview with French think tank analyst, June 19, 2015.

[92] Anton Troianovski, "Germany Seeks to Counter Russian 'Propaganda' in the Baltics," *Wall Street Journal*, April 17, 2015.

[93] Interview with EU official, June 17, 2015.

In 2015, the European Union launched a new strategic-communication effort. A decision to create a task force on communication was made at the Foreign Affairs Council in January 2015, under the aegis of the Netherlands and Nordic countries. The European Council subsequently set up a Strategic Communication Team in April 2015.[94] The purpose of this team is to counter Russian propaganda, primarily in Eastern Partnership countries (Armenia, Azerbaijan, Belarus, Georgia, Moldova, and Ukraine), by better communicating the European Union's own narrative. The idea is to explain the vision behind EU policies in nontechnical and engaging terms—on issues such as the benefits of anticorruption policies and how to access EU funds—rather than engage in counternarratives. It also purports to build a network of media representatives and civil society representatives in Eastern Partnership countries and Russia without supporting them directly, to avoid putting them at risk. The idea is to give them more visibility—a bigger platform—so that their narrative can be heard alongside the Russian "bombing" of the media.[95] Another objective of this effort is to produce documents such as audience studies to be made available to member states.[96]

Maintaining Dialogue with Russia and Avoiding Escalation

While there is agreement on a firm response to Moscow's aggressive moves, several European actors have made sure to balance this policy with a continuation of dialogue on Ukraine-related issues as well as other matters of mutual interest. This attitude may be best summarized by the French stated policy of "dialogue and firmness."[97]

---

[94] Interview with EU official, June 16, 2015; interview with EU official, June 3, 2015.

[95] Interview with EU official, June 16, 2015.

[96] Interview with EU official, June 16, 2015.

[97] See, for instance, Laurent Fabius, "La Politique Étrangère de la France: Quelle Autonomie pour Quelle Ambition?" speech before the French Senate, October 15, 2015.

The European Union, for instance, keeps a number of communication channels open while making clear that its relation with Russia is not "business as usual." One important dialogue initiated is on the implications for Russia of the implementation of the DCFTA, which is the trade component of the Association Agreement with Ukraine. The European Union postponed its provisional application until January 2016 (which includes access to the EU market) to accommodate Russian demands.[98] One EU official noted that many member states disapproved of these talks and felt that they gave Russia the upper hand.[99] The European Union has also maintained cross-border collaboration with Russia, as well as its support to Russian civil society.[100] On multilateral issues, the European Union has kept a dialogue open with Russia on Iran, Syria, the migration crisis, and ISIL, based on the notion that talking to Russia is better than isolating it and may allow for limited cooperation in areas of mutual interest.[101]

Germany, too, has been particularly supportive of maintaining a dialogue with Russia, insisting that NATO should leave open the possibility for reestablishing a positive relationship with Russia in the future.[102] German analysts interviewed pointed to a belief underlying German foreign policy that the relationship with Russia is malleable based on how Germany and the other allies choose to interact with Russia.[103] In France, there is an understanding that dialogue with Russia is needed to solve the Ukraine issue, and that isolating Russia would be even more dangerous, as it could fuel more radical forces in Russia.[104] France has suspended defense cooperation with Russia but maintained scientific, economic, and cultural cooperation—and, more

---

[98] Interview with EU official, June 15, 2015; interview with EU official, June 3, 2015; interview with EU official, June 16, 2015.

[99] Interview with EU official, June 10, 2015.

[100] Interview with EU official, June 10, 2015.

[101] Interview with EU official, June 3, 2015.

[102] Interviews with NATO officials, June 16 and 17, 2015.

[103] Interviews and discussions with German think tank analysts, June 18 and 22, 2015.

[104] Interview with French officials, June 18, 2015.

generally, any other area not affected by sanctions.[105] One particular area of continued cooperation has been counterterrorism intelligence sharing, including on issues such as Chechen networks in France and the India-Pakistan area.[106] Russia and France also share concerns about foreign fighters returning from Iraq and Syria.[107] Norway maintains technical cooperation with Russia on a number of specific areas that include the Arctic, governance of fisheries, search and rescue in the Barents Sea, and nonproliferation but has cut all high-level and military engagement with Russia.[108]

The Ukraine crisis limits the European Union's ability to engage Russia on a number of topics, including the Eurasian Union.[109] One EU official interviewed noted that "everything we say and do [in the dialogue with Russia]" stumbles on the Ukraine crisis and that "[in] our debates, we are hostage of the Ukraine crisis."[110] The European Union has closed (or excluded Russia from) a number of forums of discussion and canceled annual EU-Russia summits; EU-Russia talks on visa facilitation; and negotiations on a framework agreement encompassing all EU-Russia trade, including energy.[111] Member states, too, have suspended important bilateral meetings or summits with Russia—unless they are about solving the crisis in Ukraine.[112] This general principle,

---

[105] Interview with French government-affiliated think tank analyst, June 18, 2015; interview with French officials, June 18, 2015. The various aspects of this collaboration have been affected, however, on the Russian side by the economic crisis and the consequences of sanctions on the economy.

[106] Interview with French officials, June 18, 2015; interview with French think tank analyst, June 19, 2015.

[107] Interview with French think tank analyst, June 18, 2015; interview with French think tank analyst, June 19, 2015.

[108] Interview with Norwegian officials, July 14, 2015.

[109] Interview with EU official, June 15, 2015.

[110] Interview with EU official, June 15, 2015.

[111] Interview with EU official, June 10, 2015.

[112] Interview with EU official, June 10, 2015.

however, has been ignored by a few member states such as Greece[113] and Italy.[114]

The attempt by a number of European states to maintain dialogue with Russia also reflects a general concern that an overly military response to Russia might be seen as provocative and could lead to an escalation of the conflict.[115] A French researcher warned against "pushing Russia in a corner."[116] Similarly, Polish discussants mentioned that because so much of Russian policy is motivated by domestic factors, Putin is much more dangerous when pressed to the wall.[117] They assess that, as Putin's assertiveness in Ukraine has been building on Russian pride and the belief of many Russians that the country needed to act, many within Russia have defended the increased Russian stature even in the face of economic hardship.[118] To some extent, Western sanctions may have even reinforced Putin's position domestically by providing him with an easy scapegoat for an economic situation that is mostly to blame on Russia's structural weaknesses and overreliance on oil revenue.[119]

---

[113] Greek Prime Minister Alexis Tsipras met with Putin in Moscow in April 2015.

[114] Putin met in Rome with the Italian President and Prime Minister in June 2015.

[115] Interviews with German think tank analysts, discussions at conference, June 18 and 22, 2015.

[116] Interview with French think tank analyst, June 19, 2015.

[117] Interview with Polish official, July 13, 2015.

[118] Interview with Polish analysts, July 14, 2015.

[119] Michael Birnbaum, "A Year into a Conflict with Russia, Are Sanctions Working?" *Washington Post*, March 27, 2015.

CHAPTER FOUR

Intentions

What Is Next for Europe-Russia Relations?

European officials interviewed generally agreed on three key elements that shape their current relations with Russia, and which they believe will continue to do so in the near future. First, there is an understanding that relations with Russia have changed irremediably. There is a before and after Ukraine, as the current crisis revealed a degree of Russian assertiveness that had not been suspected previously. Second, European officials and researchers interviewed did not expect tensions with Russia to recede anytime soon. The severity of the crisis makes it likely that the crisis will be protracted, especially as Ukraine is still struggling to improve its governance and reform its economy. The alternative to such improvement—with Ukraine possibly collapsing, and with spillover effects on neighboring countries—represents a serious concern, for Poland in particular. Finally, European actions toward Russia will largely depend on Russian behavior. The European Union sees the full implementation of the Minsk II agreement as a critical benchmark that will allow them to relax the sanctions and begin rebuilding a constructive dialogue with Russia. If full implementation increasingly seems out of reach, however, there will be increased pressure on these leaders to reassess and potentially lift the sanctions.

Relations with Russia Have Changed Irremediably

Polish officials interviewed believe that a "red line has been crossed" by Russia in Crimea, in that it showed that Russia will not hesitate to use force to accomplish its objectives. This is seen by Poland as a drastic change in its strategic environment; while it is true that the risk of an invasion from Russia was always a theoretical possibility, and Polish defense planning has been keenly attentive of Russia since the regaining of full Polish sovereignty in 1989–1990, Poland now feels that its security is more at risk.[1] In the Polish view, Russia's illegal annexation of Crimea represents a permanent structural change in Russian policy that will continue beyond Putin's tenure in office due to the strong support his more assertive policies enjoy among the Russian population. This will make it difficult, if not impossible, to return to a benign security environment. Polish officials interviewed contended that, while Putin's actions are especially dangerous in the short to medium term, Russia will be unable to achieve its strategic objectives in the long term, as it has no chance of winning a confrontation with the West. The mere attempt at winning such a confrontation, however, could cause a lot of damage.[2] Similarly, in Sweden, policymakers see a fundamental change in the European security environment that is likely to persist.[3] Swedish officials interviewed consistently emphasized that Russia is unlikely to change even if Putin were to be removed from power. Most seemed to believe a return to a partnership relationship with Russia to be unlikely in the near future.[4] For example, one Swedish MP described Putin as having a "nostalgic vision" for borders roughly akin to 1914 imperial Russia; the vision accepts the loss of Finland and eastern Poland, but it still includes the Baltic States as part of its sphere of control.[5] One French official noted that France and its partners agree that there is a drastic and irreversible change in relations with Russia.[6] By making clear that the European Union and Russia have very different values

---

[1]   Interviews with Polish officials, July 13 and 14, 2015.

[2]   Interview with Polish officials, July 14, 2015.

[3]   Interviews with Swedish MP and Swedish officials, July, 2015.

[4]   Interviews with Swedish officials, July 20 and 21, 2015.

[5]   The request in June 2015 by two Russian MPs (both from Putin's United Russia party) to the Russian Chief Prosecutor's Office to examine the legality of the Baltic States' independence can also be viewed from that perspective. See "Russia Examines 1991 Recognition of Baltic Independence," BBC News, June 30, 2015; interview with Swedish MP, July 20, 2015.

[6]   Interview with French officials, June 18, 2015.

and geopolitical perspectives, the Ukrainian crisis has ensured that the relationship between Europe and Russia is unlikely to return to what was the previous "normal" anytime soon.[7]

At the NATO level, while the Wales Summit declaration maintains the goal of a future partnership with Russia, it notes that "Russia's aggressive actions against Ukraine have fundamentally challenged our vision of a Europe whole, free, and at peace."[8] NATO officials interviewed emphasized that the European security environment had comprehensively changed. One discussed Putin's intent to "break out" of and undermine the rule-based order in Europe and establish an alternative order. NATO officials traced Russia's aggressive intent back to Georgia in 2008 and explained that some planning within NATO to address a potential Russian threat had begun in 2010. One metaphor offered was that "Georgia should have been a wake-up call, but we all hit the snooze button."[9]

Tensions with Russia Are Expected to Last

Most European officials and analysts interviewed expect a protracted crisis. German analysts interviewed emphasized that Germans understand that "Russia will not get nice tomorrow" and have no specific end state in mind regarding the reestablishment of a dialogue with Russia other than trying to develop a new and as yet uncertain modus vivendi.[10] One French official expected the crisis to continue at least for the next three years because of Russia's upcoming legislative and presidential elections (in 2016 and 2018).[11] One EU official noted that disagreements and differences with Russia are unlikely to go away anytime soon; as a result, the European Union is "ready to play a long game."[12] Interviews conducted in Poland suggest that Poles believe change

---

[7] Interview with EU official, June 3, 2015; interview with EU official, June 15, 2015.

[8] NATO, 2014, para. 20 and 23.

[9] Interviews with NATO officials, June 16 and 17, 2015.

[10] Interview with think tank analyst, June 18, 2015.

[11] Interview with French officials, June 18, 2015.

[12] Interview with EU official, June 3, 2015.

under Putin is unlikely and that there is little prospect for significant changes to take place for at least a dozen years—maybe more. Poles fear that, if Ukraine does not receive greater Western support, the situation will further deteriorate. Expectations are that, since dividing the West has not worked so far, Putin wants to freeze the conflict and keep Ukraine on the verge of collapse so that it is not an attractive partner for the West and remains part of Russia's sphere of influence. Russian policy has therefore focused on subversion of Ukraine, with the goal of installing a government that would be more friendly toward Russia and subordinate to Russian interests.[13] Finally, many European officials believe that the goal of Russian policy is to consolidate Russian control over states located in the former Soviet space—a group with Ukraine at its core.[14] According to this view, what happened in Crimea is the expression of a coherent and sustained Russian policy designed to keep Ukraine and other post-Soviet states in Russia's sphere of influence (at least economically, if not politically). Russia also seeks to establish itself as an equal partner to the major European powers, rather than interacting with the Euro-Atlantic institutions, as shown, for instance, by its insistence on the Normandy format for negotiations on Ukraine.[15]

Russia's Behavior Will Condition Europe's Behavior

The actions Europeans take with regard to Russia will largely depend on Russia's behavior. The Wales Summit declaration also mentions such conditionality:

> The nature of the Alliance's relations with Russia and our aspiration for partnership will be contingent on our seeing a clear, constructive change in Russia's actions which demonstrates compliance with international law and its international obligations and responsibilities.[16]

---

[13]   Interview with Polish official, July 14, 2015.

[14]   Interview with Polish officials, July 13, 2015.

[15]   Interview with Polish official, July 13, 2015.

[16]   NATO, 2014, para. 20 and 23.

Such conditionality is also a key element of the EU sanctions policy, which can be adjusted up and down depending on Russian behavior.[17] Economic sanctions are presently linked to the full implementation of the Minsk II agreement, suggesting that Russia's failure to abide by the agreement could lead to broader sanctions—assuming all EU members can still agree on this issue—or economic sanctions will almost certainly be reconsidered if Russia complies.[18]

Conditioning one's actions on Russia's might also be necessary from a domestic politics perspective. A significant portion of the German popular opinion supports exclusively a diplomatic solution to the crisis. Thus, the extent to which it would be politically feasible for Europeans to pursue further military responses to Russia's actions in Ukraine will heavily depend on how clear it is that Russia has violated key agreements and international law.[19]

A number of "red lines" could trigger stronger reactions from European countries. Polish officials noted that, if Russia were to launch a major military operation in Ukraine, the West could no longer evade adopting a clear course of action. Such an operation could potentially open up the prospect of providing lethal aid to Ukraine.[20] One French official hypothesized that, if separatists took over Mariupol, Kharkiv, or Odessa (obviously with Russian support, since they would not be able to seize such territory on their own), this would probably trigger additional sanctions by the European Union. This interviewee believed, however, that Putin is unlikely to make such a move, since he has already reached his objective, which was to destabilize Ukraine.[21] A Finnish official similarly maintained that a Russian offensive in

---

[17] Interview with EU official, June 10, 2015; interview with EU official, June 16, 2015.

[18] Interview with EU official, June 3, 2015; interview with EU official, June 16, 2015.

[19] Interviews with German think tank analysts, discussions at conference, June 18 and 22, 2015.

[20] Interview with Polish officials, July 14, 2015.

[21] Interview with French government-affiliated think tank analyst, June 18, 2015. Two more French researchers interviewed did not expect Russia to attempt to extend its territorial gains in Ukraine (interview with French government-affiliated think tank analyst, June 19, 2015; interview with French think tank analyst, June 19, 2015).

Ukraine would trigger stronger measures.[22] In the event of a Russian-supported attack against their territory, Estonian and Latvian officials made it quite clear that their governments intend to respond and try to defeat Russian, or Russian-backed, forces. They recognized their responsibility as first responders to any Russian assault and emphasized that they would immediately seek greater assistance from NATO.[23] There is, however, no official "red line" for the European Union and most European governments. One EU official noted that, if such a red line were made public, it could encourage Russia to take advantage of it and would also limit the EU's flexibility in calibrating a response.[24]

Sustaining Existing Measures and Planning for New Ones

Assistance to Ukraine

Assistance to Ukraine appears to be one of the most widely agreed measures likely to be pursued in the future. Interviewees in Sweden emphasized the need to help Ukraine through both financial aid and technical assistance.[25] In Brussels and Berlin, our interlocutors confirmed strong support for the EU Civilian Security Sector Assistance Mission, contrary to the questions in Kyiv about the European Union's hesitant attitude toward the mission.[26] Ukraine may, however, soon experience the effects of donor fatigue, especially as other countries in Europe require help as well. One French analyst noted that France lacks the means to support Ukraine financially, as its budget constraints limit the amount of assistance it can render at the same time it is assisting Greece.[27] While many NATO officials admitted that the Minsk II agreement was unlikely to succeed, they noted that there had

---

[22]   Interview with Finnish official, May 28, 2015.

[23]   Interview with Estonian and Latvian officials, July 15 and 17, 2015.

[24]   Interview with EU official, June 16, 2015.

[25]   Interviews with Swedish officials, July 20 and 21, 2015.

[26]   Interview with foreign official working in Ukraine, May 2015.

[27]   Interview with French think tank analyst, June 18, 2015.

been no significant discussions of what to do if the agreement were to break down.[28]

Sanctions

Several countries have expressed doubts on the usefulness of sanctions, including Hungary, Italy, Bulgaria, the Czech Republic, and Slovakia; one EU official described the EU consensus on this issue as "not going without difficulty."[29] EU officials interviewed in Brussels in June 2015 had no doubt that the sanctions would be prolonged without difficulty later that month—and indeed they were.[30] President of the EU Council Donald Tusk has played an important role maintaining consensus among the 28 members through consultations and negotiations supplemented by behind-the-scenes negotiations by powerful EU players such as Germany.[31] So far, the method has worked, as the consensus was maintained despite the 28 members' widely different understandings of what Russia's actions mean for their own security and their suffering, to various degrees, from the impact of the sanctions and countersanctions on their own economies.

Another reason sanctions are likely to be maintained is that they are generally seen as having an impact on Russia.[32] Even though this impact is difficult to evaluate—Russian economic difficulties are also largely due to other factors, such as the decline in oil prices and the structural weaknesses of the Russian economy—it is worth noting that entities listed on the sanctions list have not been able to obtain financial assistance to ease the economic strains imposed by the sanctions, and some Russian entities have brought legal challenges to the European Union. Both developments suggest that Russia is feeling the pain from

---

[28] Interviews with NATO officials, June 15 and 16, 2015.

[29] Interview with EU official, June 10, 2015; interview with EU official, June 3, 2015.

[30] Interview with EU official, June 10, 2015; interview with EU official, June 3, 2015.

[31] Interview with EU official, June 10, 2015.

[32] Interview with EU official, June 10, 2015; Edward Hunter Christie, "Sanctions After Crimea: Have They Worked?" *NATO Review*, undated; Ina Dreyer and Nicu Popescu, "Do Sanctions Against Russia Work?" European Union Institute for Security Studies, Brief Issue No. 35, December 2014; Birnbaum, 2015.

the sanctions,[33] although this does not mean that Russia will change its behavior as a result. One EU official called sanctions the EU's "deterrence tool" and believes they have prevented Russia from taking more aggressive steps.[34]

European governments do not seem to face excessive pressure domestically to end sanctions, even though some countries have been disproportionately hurt by the EU sanctions and Russia's countersanctions policies. A few EU members have experienced some economic disruptions in sectors heavily dependent on the Russian market; for instance, Latvian exports of smoked sprats (sardine-like fish popular in the Baltic Sea region) have been hit hard by the Russian embargo, and Latvia has sought to locate alternative markets.[35] Nevertheless, despite some concern regarding the economic impact on certain industries, there is little sign that any of the Baltic States will soften its policy toward Russia given the perception of a continued Russian threat. One interlocutor explained that Latvian businesses recognize the risk of doing business with Russia.[36] In Germany, analysts and officials interviewed generally contended that there was limited pressure from the business community to end the sanctions. Several interviewees referred to a letter from the Bundesverband der Deutschen Industrie, the German trade association, in support of the sanctions.[37] One Finnish official mentioned an opinion poll on perceptions regarding the sanctions carried out in the spring of 2015 among Finnish companies. While these companies (milk and dairy producers, in particular) are suffering from Russia's countersanctions, most showed strong support for the sanctions policy. According to this official, this is because of a

---

[33]   Interview with EU official, June 16, 2015.

[34]   Interview with EU official, June 17, 2015.

[35]   Interview with foreign officials based in Riga, July 16, 2015.

[36]   Interview with Latvian academic, July 15, 2015.

[37]   Interviews with German official and academic, June 19, 2015.

widely shared understanding, based on the memory of the 1939–1940 Winter War, that "vis-à-vis Russia you need to be tough."[38]

Yet, it remains unclear whether the consensus will hold if the situation in Ukraine stagnates. In January 2016, for instance, Italy delayed the decision to renew sanctions, asking for further discussions on the matter. Its opposition to Germany's support for the Nord Stream 2 gas pipeline project—an opposition echoed, to some extent, by Tusk—exposed the tensions that exist within the European Union on sanctions, as well as more broadly on policy toward Russia.[39]

Military Options

With regard to military options, one French analyst noted that France could reinforce the current reassurance measures were Russia to become more aggressive, but it would hardly be in a position to pursue further military options.[40] One official similarly noted how difficult it was for France to conduct a credible (and sustainable) deterrent policy in a period of constrained defense budgets. The permanent force deployments that Poland and the Baltic States are asking for, in particular, are deemed unrealistic considering France's budget.[41]

Air-policing missions over the Baltic States, which represent a key element of NATO's reassurance measures toward its easternmost members, were reduced in September 2015. The number of aircraft deployed for policing the borders of the Baltic States declined from 16 to eight in response to a decrease in airspace violations from Russia. While NATO stated that eight was the current requirement, it also

---

[38] Interview with Finnish official, May 28, 2015. This official also noted that countersanctions have affected the Finnish economy much less than other trends in the Russian economy, such as the decrease in oil prices, the diminished value of the ruble, and the general lack of reforms in the Russian economy. All these trends had resulted in a contraction of Finnish exports to Russia starting in 2013, i.e., before the Ukraine crisis.

[39] Kanter, 2015.

[40] Interview with French think tank analyst, June 18, 2015.

[41] Interview with French officials, June 18, 2015.

noted that the number of aircraft might surge again if the security situation required it.[42]

Our interlocutors saw the provision of lethal aid as unlikely in the near future, considering that this option is generally unpopular in Europe.[43] One analyst in France outlined that it could lead to an escalation of the conflict and a massive influx of Ukrainian refugees.[44] Another French researcher described such lethal aid as a "gift" to Putin, as it would support his claims that the West is the aggressor.[45] Yet, French public opinion seems more supportive of the idea, with 40 percent of respondents supporting NATO sending arms to Ukraine—compared with 46 percent in the United States, 25 percent in Spain, 22 percent in Italy, and 19 percent in Germany.[46] German officials remain committed to strengthening governance in Ukraine, though any sort of direct military assistance is "off the table."[47] Opposition to providing lethal arms to Ukraine is particularly strong in Germany. Individuals surveyed expressed the strongest hostility to NATO sending arms to the Ukrainian government, with 77 percent opposing such a policy. Poland and the United Kingdom are the only European countries (out of six surveyed) where disapproval of providing lethal arms to Ukraine is less than 50 percent. It is worth noting, however, that support for sending arms to Ukraine is low overall—it reaches 50 percent in Poland, and, in the United States, only 46 percent approve of the measure (see Figure 4.1).

---

[42] John Vandiver, "NATO: Fewer Flights Needed to Patrol Baltic Airspace," *Stars and Stripes*, August 5, 2015; "NATO Halves Baltic Air Policing Mission," Agence France-Presse, August 4, 2015. Prior to 2014, the Baltic Air Policing Mission typically involved only four aircraft from a single nation (Nicholas de Larrinaga, "NATO's Tripled Baltic Air Policing Mission Begins," *Jane's Defence Weekly*, April 30, 2014).

[43] Discussions with Polish and Swedish officials, July 13–14, 20–21, 2015.

[44] Interview with French think tank analyst, June 19, 2015.

[45] Interview with French think tank analyst, June 18, 2015.

[46] Simmons, Stokes, and Poushter, 2015, p. 4.

[47] Interviews and discussions with think tank analysts, June 18 and 22, 2015. Several analysts noted that Germany had supplied antitank weapons to the Kurdish forces in Iraq but not to Ukraine (interviews with German think tank analysts and academic, June 18 and 19, 2015).

Figure 4.1
Percentage of Respondents Who Oppose NATO Sending Arms to the Ukrainian Government

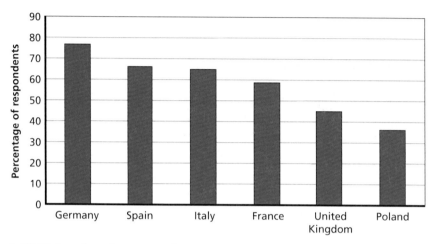

SOURCE: Data from Simmons, Stokes, and Poushter, 2015, p. 52.
RAND RR1579-4.1

General discomfort with military options can also be seen in the debate about permanently deployed forces. At the Wales Summit, Germany insisted that the Alliance's policy not undermine the NATO-Russia Founding Act. The alternative policy of enhanced rotation of NATO forces and strengthening NATO's capacity for rapid response were more closely in line with Germany's perception of how to achieve reassurance and deterrence without provoking Russia.[48]

Any discussion of developing or deploying German military forces to respond to Russian aggression appears politically difficult in Germany, especially given the history of Nazi occupation of eastern Europe.[49] It remains easier for German officials to focus on nonmilitary threats from Russia, such as strategic communication, Russia's threat to liberal values, and its manipulation of economic instruments. On the German left, opinions are divided. Elements of the Green party have adopted

---

[48] Interviews with NATO officials, June 15–17, 2015.

[49] Interviews with German think tank analysts, official, and academic, June 18 and 19, 2015.

the most hawkish policy because of Russia's record on human rights. The Die Linke party, and a larger group of "Russian-sympathizers" (*Russlandversteher*) within Germany, however, maintain an affinity for Russia and believe that the country has been misunderstood.[50] Many on the German left remain suspicious of NATO as a military organization and believe that NATO's revisionist goals provoked Russian aggression.[51] German analysts also emphasize that there is a major elite-versus-mass divide. While SPD officials may have become more critical of Russia since the beginning of the crisis, the popular opinion still supports the possibility of partnership with Russia and blames NATO for provoking the conflict.[52] Finally, several German analysts note a growing consensus that Germany should play a greater role in defending the international order, but there is no clear understanding of how this will be put into practice.[53] Despite internal disagreements about a greater military role, at the Warsaw Summit, Germany did agree to become a framework nation supporting the new forward deployed battalion in Lithuania.[54]

Germany's attitude stands in sharp contrast to Poland's, where our interlocutors believed that weakness was deeply problematic in dealing with Russia and invited aggressive Russian behavior. There was visible dismay among them about any discussion of limiting NATO's response to avoid provoking Russia. The Poles see recent Russian maneuvers involving massive numbers of troops as an attempt by Russia to influence policies in the Baltic States. They claim that, if there is not a firm response to such intimidation, it will be seen by Russia as a sign of weakness, and as a sign of success of Russian policy.[55] In that regard, the lesson Polish officials and analysts draw from the Ukrainian crisis

---

[50]   Interview with German academic, June 19, 2015.

[51]   Interview with German think tank representatives, June 18, 2015.

[52]   Interviews with German think tank analysts and academic, June 18 and 19, 2015.

[53]   Interviews with German official and academic, June 19, 2015. (The discussion about how Germany should adapt itself in the future is happening in the context of its white paper, which will outline its overall defense strategy into the near future.)

[54]   NATO, 2016, para. 40.

[55]   Interview with a Polish official, July 13, 2015.

is that weakness invites trouble and is dangerous. They believe that Ukraine was weak and unable to defend itself, which made it a magnet for Russian subversion.[56] Consequently, NATO must show decisiveness and resolve and remain united as one organization that provides security for all members.[57] Polish officials interviewed expressed regret that the era when NATO concentrated on out-of-area missions was used by many NATO states to reduce defense budgets, capabilities, and forces, resulting in the virtual disarmament of previously militarily strong states, foremost Germany.[58]

Will European States Increase Their Defense Spending?

The perception that the Ukrainian crisis has irremediably altered European security perspectives—turning Russia into a strategic adversary rather than a partner—has provided new impetus to the debate in individual European countries on whether their defense spending is adequate to address current and future security threats. Such a debate exists also at the EU level, on the capabilities that the union can or should have in a domain—defense—not central to its identity.

The Stockholm International Peace Research Institute (SIPRI)'s study of trends in military spending reveals that, between 2013 and 2014, military expenses increased in eastern Europe (Russia and its immediate neighbors) by 8.4 percent, while they decreased in western and central Europe by 1.9 percent.[59] The largest increases were for Ukraine (a 23-percent increase)[60] and Poland (13-percent increase), fol-

---

[56]   Interview with Polish analysts, July 14, 2015.

[57]   Interview with Polish officials, July 14, 2015.

[58]   Interview with Polish official, July 13, 2015.

[59]   These fit in larger trends—a 98-percent increase for eastern Europe and an 8.3-percent decrease in western and central Europe since 2005. See SIPRI, *Trends in World Military Expenditure 2014*, fact sheet, April 2015, p. 4. SIPRI defines eastern Europe as comprising Armenia, Azerbaijan, Belarus, Georgia, Moldova, Ukraine, and Russia (SIPRI, "Regional Coverage," database, undated.)

[60]   This figure is marked as "uncertain estimate" (SIPRI, 2015, p. 4).

lowed by Russia and Lithuania (respectively, 8.1 percent and 6 percent). SIPRI further noted that "[i]ncreases in many Central European countries, as well as some of the Nordic countries, are likely to continue in 2015, in part as a reaction to the crisis in Ukraine."[61] This is certainly the case in Sweden, where the developments in Ukraine have led to a policy that combines increasing defense spending and intensifying cooperation with neighbors and NATO, with the implicit goal of ensuring a measure of collective defense.[62] Swedish reactions to Russian aggression in Ukraine have been compounded by a growing realization of increasing Swedish military weakness. Many in Sweden were surprised by claims by the SACEUR in 2013 that, at best, Sweden could hold out against a Russian attack for only one week.[63] Prior to 2014, there was a consensus regarding downsizing the military and orienting Swedish forces around crisis response and contributions to international missions, which was based on a belief that there were no major military threats in the region. Economic challenges encouraged a decline in military expenditures.[64] This has changed. The most recent Swedish defense bill for the period from 2016 to 2020 calls for a relatively modest 2.2 percent increase in spending year over year—or $722 million over five years.[65] The defense bill, the result of an agreement by Sweden's five main parties, also calls for a return to a policy of "total defense" involving both civilian and military personnel; station-

---

[61] SIPRI, 2015, p. 4.

[62] Interviews with Swedish officials, July 21, 2015.

[63] Ford, 2014.

[64] A center-right coalition, including the Liberal and Moderate parties, supported continued decline in military expenditure before they left the government in the last election. Analysts explain that they sought to gain votes from the left-leaning Swedes (interviews with Swedish analysts and journalists, July 20–21, 2015).

[65] "Swedish Defense Bill 2016–2020," Government Offices of Sweden, April 24, 2015; Charlie Duxbury, "Sweden Plans to Increase Military Spending," Wall Street Journal, March 12, 2015.

ing two battalions of ground forces on Gotland; and improving the navy and air force.[66]

In Germany, public opinion is increasingly amenable to greater military spending, particularly after a series of scandals questioned the efficiency and reliability of the German military. Poor maintenance, unreliable equipment, and other technical problems appear to be embarrassing even to pacifist Germans. One of our interlocutors noted that, while many foreign-policy elites had assumed that there would be little interest among Germans in increasing military spending, an October 2014 survey showed more support than expected, with 55 percent of respondents supporting such an increase for the Bundeswehr (the unified armed forces of Germany) in the medium term.[67]

A French official believed France's defense budget is unlikely to increase further in the current economic context, especially as France is the only European country already engaged militarily at a high level around the world—suggesting that France will nudge its European partners to do more before it increases its own spending.[68] In response to the January 2015 terrorist attack in Paris, the French Parliament updated the 2015–2019 Military Planning Law to reduce planned personnel cuts from 30,000 to 15,000 and increase operational forces in the Army from 66,000 to 77,000.[69] One researcher believed that "the paradigm has changed," as a number of new threats (ISIL, jihadist groups in the Sahel, terrorist attacks on French soil, Ukraine) could reverse the downward trend in defense spending and justify an increase in defense expenditures.[70] The November 2015 attack resulted in French

---

[66] The Social Democratic Party, Moderate Party, Green Party, Centre Party, and Christian Democrats ("Swedish Defense Bill 2016–2020," 2015).

[67] Infratest dimap, *ARD-DeutschlandTREND*, survey report, October 2014; interviews with German official and academic, June 19, 2015.

[68] Interview with French officials, June 18, 2015.

[69] Interview with French officials, June 18, 2015.

[70] Interview with French think tank analyst, June 18, 2015.

lawmakers increasing the funds for the Defense Ministry (among other security-related measures) by another 200 million euros.[71]

Among Nordic countries, Finland's defense policy has been to emphasize readiness—the country is unusual in Europe in that it has retained conscription and a large reserve force that maintains high combat potential.[72] The Finnish Army is also working on possibly adding a new quick-reaction force, with a short timeline for mobilization.[73] In Norway, the general attitude as of mid-2015 was toward an increase in defense spending, partly based on the crisis with Russia.[74] A few months later, it was announced that the 2016 budget for Norwegian armed forces would rise to $6 billion, or 1.54 percent of Norway's gross domestic product—a 9.8-percent increase compared with 2015.[75]

The Baltic States intend to continue to develop their forces, seek a greater U.S. presence, and increase their defense spending for the first time since the global financial crisis.[76] Estonia appears to be identifying and addressing flaws in its preparedness. Latvian officials and analysts are clearly concerned about the country's low defense budget, and there was an uptick in spending in 2015.[77] In July 2015, Latvia and Lithuania announced that they would increase their defense budget to 2 percent and 1.5 percent of their gross domestic products, respectively.[78]

As for military responses at the EU level, the Union is exploring potential avenues for action. One would be improving the European Union's ability to provide military equipment to partner nations. Cur-

[71] "Après les Attentats, le Budget 2016 Prévoit 815 Millions d'Euros pour les Mesures de Sécurité," *Le Monde*, November 30, 2015.

[72] Interview with Finnish official, May 28, 2015.

[73] Interview with Finnish official, July 14, 2015.

[74] Interview with Norwegian officials, July 14, 2015.

[75] Gerard O'Dwyer, "9.8% Budget Hike Set for Norwegian Armed Forces," *Defense News*, October 9, 2015c.

[76] SIPRI, 2015, p. 4.

[77] Interviews with Latvian officials, former government official, and foreign contractor working in Riga, July 15, 2015.

[78] Jaroslaw Adamowski, "Latvia, Lithuania to Raise Defense Spending," *Defense News*, July 30, 2015.

rently, provision of military equipment is not considered a Common Security and Defense Policy (CSDP) matter in spite of the European Union's rising involvement in nation and institution building.[79] To address this gap, the High Representative for Foreign Affairs and Security Policy and the Commission issued a Joint Communication in April 2015 on "[c]apacity-building in support of security and development—enabling partners to prevent and manage crises."[80] Although the discussion on this issue is only starting, the European Union may, in the near future, incorporate the provision of military equipment to the CSDP, or it could develop a dedicated instrument to train and equip partners.[81] An alternative solution would be opening access to existing funds for such purposes. For instance, the Instrument contributing to Stability and Peace, administered by the Commission and defined as "the main instrument supporting security initiatives and peace-building activities in partner countries,"[82] cannot currently fund programs whose recipients are military.[83] The Ukrainian crisis may provide some impetus to alter EU processes in ways that would make the Union more capable of playing a military—in addition to diplomatic and economic—role in the resolution of the crisis.

---

[79] Interview with EU official, June 17, 2015.

[80] This document notes, for instance, that

> the EU's comprehensive approach needs to be strengthened to cover gaps in the current EU response. For example, this may be the case where training has been provided by Common Security and Defence Policy (CSDP) missions, but its sustainability and effectiveness has been hampered by a lack of basic partner country equipment" (European Commission and High Representative of the European Union for Foreign Affairs and Security Policy, "Capacity Building in Support of Security and Development—Enabling Partners to Prevent and Manage Crises," Joint Communication to the European Parliament and the Council JOIN[2015] 17, Brussels, April 28, 2015).

[81] Interview with EU official, June 17, 2015; Thierry Tardy, "Enabling Partners to Manage Crises: From 'Train and Equip' to Capacity-Building," European Union Institute for Security Studies Brief Issue No. 18, June 2015.

[82] Directorate General for International Cooperation and Development, "The Instrument contributing to Stability and Peace (IcSP)," Brussels, European Commission, undated.

[83] Interview with EU official, June 17, 2015.

Even without clear military capabilities, the European Union has gathered, through its CSDP missions, extensive experience in building civilian capabilities of foreign nations, and such capabilities could be brought to support NATO's effort. French officials interviewed believed that, in the crisis with Russia, the paramilitary police and border guards Ukraine needs could particularly benefit from this experience.[84] This, however, leaves open the question of the modalities under which EU capabilities could be employed by NATO, especially as cooperation between the two institutions has been uneven.[85] One EU official also pointed to the Union's ability to offer comprehensive solutions that rely on different instruments. For instance, antipiracy Operation Atalanta,[86] in the Indian Ocean, included military training (EU Training Mission), civilian training (European Union Regional Maritime Capacity Building for the Horn of Africa and the Western Indian Ocean), capacity-building programs for the judiciary sector and coast guard (among others), and development assistance.[87] Finally, the crisis with Russia has given new impetus to the debate about a common European defense policy and possibly, in the longer term, a European Army. President of the European Commission Jean-Claude Juncker called in March 2015 for a European Army to show Russia that the European Union can defend its values and respond to threats against

---

[84] A recent example of such EU training is the European Union Border Assistance Mission in Libya, which supports in particular the Libyan customs and Naval Coast Guard (see EEAS, "Common Security and Defence Policy: EU Integrated Border Assistance Mission in Libya (EUBAM Libya)," fact sheet, January 2015; and Andrew Rettman, "EU 'Civilian' Mission Training Paramilitaries in Libya," *EUObserver*, November 18, 2013).

[85] Conversation with French officials, May 12, 2015. See also Karl-Heinz Kamp, "NATO-EU Cooperation: Forget It!" *Strategic Europe* blog, Carnegie Europe, October 30, 2013; Kristin Archick, "The European Union: Questions and Answers," Congressional Research Service, January 19, 2016, pp. 7–8.

[86] Also known as EU Naval Force Somalia—Operation Atalanta. See EU Naval Force Somalia, "Countering Piracy off the Coast of Somalia," fact sheet, undated.

[87] Interview with EU official, June 17, 2015.

its members or neighbors.[88] This idea received the support of German Minister of Defense Ursula von der Leyen, who acknowledged, however, that such a project was unrealistic in the short to medium term.[89]

Implications for NATO

Reform

NATO officials interviewed gave the impression that the European allies will further develop military responses to Russia. As one noted, "no one is arguing for less . . . [there are] reservations about whether it is enough, or whether people are willing to pay for it."[90] In the immediate term, NATO will continue to develop the NRF and other measures specified in the RAP. Discussions about the details of how forces would be allocated to the VJTF, for example, are still ongoing, though there is progress in setting up an interim VJTF.[91] One NATO official observed that, in practical terms, the NATO-Russia Founding Act was no longer constraining the NATO response, as the member states might individually choose to have a forward presence even if the Alliance does not.[92] There was also a consensus that the Alliance's posture toward Russia would be strengthened at the Warsaw Summit in 2016—as it indeed was, with the announcement of a further deployment of 4,000 troops in the Baltic States and Poland.[93] One fundamental issue for the Alliance's future response is how costs of any deployment will be shared. To date, costs for military actions "fall where they lie," meaning that whatever nation provides the military capabilities also pays the associ-

---

[88] Interview of Jean-Claude Juncker (Beat Balzli, Christoph B. Schiltz, and André Tauber, "Halten Sie sich an Frau Merkel. Ich Mache das!" *Die Welt*, March 8, 2015).

[89] "Face à la Russie, Jean-Claude Juncker Veut une Armée Européenne," *L'Express* and Agence France-Presse, March 8, 2015.

[90] Interviews with NATO official, June 15, 2015.

[91] Interviews with NATO and foreign officials, June 15, 2015.

[92] Interview with NATO official, June 17, 2015.

[93] Jaroslaw Adamowski, "NATO Agrees on E European Rotational Troops at Warsaw Summit," *Defense News*, July 8, 2016.

ated costs. This makes additional contributions from more western and southern member states politically difficult, since these countries feel that there is less of a threat from Russia yet are being asked to contribute forces and associated resources.[94]

Our discussions also revealed certain areas where NATO efforts could be improved. NATO headquarters is taking action to assess and improve the Alliance's decisionmaking, but the sharing and analysis of indicators and warnings also needs to be improved. Given the Alliance's dependence on responsiveness, it is essential for the Alliance to be able to quickly develop a shared picture of Russian activity. With further attention to implementation, current intelligence-sharing capabilities and procedures do appear to meet this requirement. Further, our interlocutors emphasized the need for more discussion about the Alliance's policy on nuclear deterrence, especially given Russia's increasing rhetoric in this area.[95] Finally, several interlocutors mentioned that issues such as energy security and strategic communication might benefit from greater cooperation between the European Union and NATO.[96]

Enlargement

Some of the NATO officials interviewed noted that members of the Alliance were divided along geographic lines about the future accession of Georgia, Ukraine, and Moldova. While NATO has consistently emphasized that the Alliance will retain its open door policy, the more-western countries fear that the enlargement of NATO will be regarded as a provocative step by Russia and exacerbate tensions with Russia. Eastern members, by contrast, tend to believe that admitting new members to the Alliance will deter Russia from taking aggressive actions that challenge the independence and sovereignty of Alliance

---

[94]   Interviews with NATO officials, June 15, 2015.

[95]   Interviews with NATO officials, June 15–17, 2015.

[96]   However, continuing political difficulties related to Cyprus prevent effective coordination between the European Union and NATO (interviews with NATO officials, June 15, 2015; interviews with German think tank analysts, June 18, 2015). See also Judy Dempsey, "Time to End the EU-NATO Standoff," *Strategic Europe* blog, Carnegie Europe, December 8, 2014.

members.[97] Given these differing viewpoints among the Alliance members, in the current strategic environment, there is no near-term realistic prospect for membership for Georgia, Ukraine, or Moldova. In Sweden, another country that is not a member of the Alliance, support for joining NATO has substantially increased over the past ten years.[98] In October 2014, the number of supporters of NATO membership outnumbered opponents for the first time (37 to 36 percent).[99] In September 2015, the volte-face of the Center party, traditionally an opponent of Sweden's membership in NATO, brought public support for NATO membership to a new height—41 percent.[100] Most opposition parties (Liberals, Moderates, and Christian Democrats, in addition to the Center) have a pro-NATO policy.[101] Newspapers associated with these parties regularly note the fundamental contradiction in Sweden's policy of paying the costs of partnership with NATO without receiving the formal benefits of collective defense. A number of Swedish analysts interviewed see Sweden as a "security hole" in northern Europe and fault Sweden for failing to uphold its responsibilities towards its eastern neighbors, which joining NATO might help correct.[102]

However, the issue of NATO membership remains divisive domestically. Left-wing parties (including the Social Democrats and Greens) generally oppose joining NATO and would rather build up Sweden's capabilities through conscription and preserve the country's tradition of neutrality.[103] Several of our interlocutors observed, however,

---

[97] Interviews with NATO officials, June 15, 2015.

[98] See, for instance, Erik Lindblad, "The Future of Sweden's Partnership with NATO," paper, Sciences-Po (Paris School of International Affairs) and Institut de Recherche Stratégique de l'Ecole Militaire, Spring 2014, p. 8.

[99] "Poll Shows More Swedes in Favor of NATO for First Time," Reuters, October 29, 2014.

[100] Gerard O'Dwyer, "New Poll Shows Sharp Shift in NATO Support," *Defense News*, September 17, 2015b.

[101] O'Dwyer, 2015b.

[102] Interviews with Swedish think tank analysts and journalists, July 20, 2015.

[103] Conscription is seen as a desirable means of maintaining a close connection between the society and military and preventing misuse of the military (interviews with Swedish think tank analysts and journalists, July 20, 2015).

that Sweden's "neutrality" was often misunderstood.[104] While Swedish governments pursued a policy of neutrality during the Cold War and criticized U.S. actions in Vietnam and other theaters of conflict, in practice, there was significant cooperation between Sweden and the United States. On the far right, the Swedish Democrats recognize the threat posed by Russia and strongly oppose NATO and the European Union, preferring to develop a strong national defense by reappropriating funds currently spent on recent immigrants.[105]

In Finland, the government decided even before the Ukrainian crisis broke out to spend more resources on training and exercising with NATO.[106] The trend toward support for NATO membership, however, is less clear than in Sweden. This might be because of the consensus between the president, the government, and the armed forces that there is no need to join NATO at the moment. An opinion poll, however, showed that if all three institutions said that Finland should join NATO, then a majority of the population would vote in favor of membership at a referendum.[107] In addition, the government formed after the April 2015 parliamentary elections made the decision to start looking at the pros and cons of NATO membership.[108] Like Sweden, Finland is very much aligned militarily with the West, even without being a member of the Alliance. The Soviet Union curtailed Finland's sovereignty during the Cold War, and the country was a Soviet-leaning "neutral." Consequently, during the Cold War, Finland balanced its military procurement between the East, the West, and its domestic

---

[104] Elizabeth Pond, "Secrets of the Baltic: Swedish Cold War Neutrality Revisited," *World Policy* blog, September 26, 2012.

[105] Interviews with Swedish think tank analysts and journalists, July 20, 2015.

[106] Interview with Finnish official, July 14, 2015.

[107] Technically, a referendum is not a necessity, since the decision to join NATO could simply be taken by the parliament. However, it would be politically difficult for any government to push such an important measure through parliament without putting it first to a popular vote. The results of a referendum would not be binding, although it is hard to imagine the parliament not abiding by these results. Finland has had two referendums in the past: one in 1931 to abolish the prohibition of alcohol, and one in 1994 on EU membership (interview with Finnish official, May 28, 2015).

[108] Interview with Finnish official, May 28, 2015.

production. Since the collapse of the Union of Soviet Socialist Republics, Finland moved quickly toward alignment with the West, and now its entire equipment follows NATO standards. Finland has deepened its defense cooperation at the bilateral level (e.g., with Sweden and the United States) and regionally, with NORDEFCO, the European Union, and NATO.

Sweden and Finland are two of the five countries that benefit from an enhanced NATO partnership (Enhanced Opportunities Partners program) that was announced at the Wales Summit.[109] Both countries have also signed host-nation support agreements with NATO, which will make it easier for them to host or serve as transit points for allied forces, including for training and exercises.[110] This agreement facilitates cooperation activities that in the past were largely ad hoc. Sweden and Finland see the agreement as an opportunity to do more NATO exercises and training and to be involved in the discussions leading to decisions made by NATO members only.[111]

Besides the uncertainty of a referendum on NATO membership and some level of domestic opposition, a major reason Finland and Sweden will likely remain on the threshold of membership is the connection of their memberships. A decision by Sweden to join the Alliance alone would isolate Finland, which would lose the benefits of close Swedish-Finnish cooperation and become more vulnerable to potential Russian pressure. Both countries joining together would be problematic as well, since Russia would see Finnish accession as an offensive measure—as Russian officials already made clear to Finland.[112] Finland has significant military capabilities, and the Finnish-Russian border is

---

[109] The other three countries were Australia, Georgia, and Jordan.

[110] See "Finland and Sweden Sign Memorandum of Understanding with NATO," press release, NATO SHAPE Public Affairs Office, September 5, 2014; and Gerard O'Dwyer, "Sweden and Finland Pursue 'Special Relationship' with NATO," *Defense News*, October 10, 2014. Such a possibility existed and had been employed before, but the memorandum of understanding formalized it. As a Finnish official put it, it "gives a standardized way of doing things, and each side knows what is expected. It makes life easier" (interview with Finnish official, July 14, 2015).

[111] Interview with Finnish official, July 14, 2015.

[112] Interview with Finnish official, May 28, 2015.

close (approximately 100 miles) to Russia's second-largest metropolitan area (St. Petersburg), which would reinforce the Russian perception of encirclement if Finland joined NATO.[113] Overall, given the risks of Finland's accession, and the continuing questions about the popularity of NATO and breaking Sweden's tradition of neutrality, any move toward NATO membership appears unlikely in the near future.

Implications for the European Union's Eastern Neighborhood

EU officials interviewed appeared confident that what happened in Ukraine[114] would not discourage those countries close to Russia and part of the European Neighborhood Policy (ENP)[115] from building a stronger relationship with the European Union.[116] One noted that Georgia's, Armenia's, and even Ukraine's interest in the European Union had remained unchanged after the crisis.[117] Some countries even showed disappointment after the Riga Summit of May 2015, when no promises of membership were made.[118] The official consensus in Brussels remains that, as long as Eastern Partnership members undertake reforms, membership is always a possibility in the long term.[119]

Yet, prospects for enlargement were limited to begin with. EU member states suffer from "enlargement fatigue," with populations increasingly skeptical of the European Union's ability to integrate newcomers successfully, particularly in a context where some existing members—e.g., Greece—require substantial assistance from others.

---

[113] Interviews with Swedish MP, think tank analysts, and journalists, July 20 and 21, 2015.

[114] It was Ukrainian President Viktor Yanukovych's decision in March 2014 not to sign the Association Agreement with the European Union that prompted the popular demonstrations known as "Euromaidan" and, eventually, the demise of the regime.

[115] Belarus, Ukraine, Moldova, Georgia, Azerbaijan, and Armenia.

[116] Interview with EU official, June 10, 2015; interview with EU official, June 3, 2015.

[117] Interview with EU official, June 3, 2015.

[118] Interview with EU official, June 10, 2015.

[119] Interview with EU official, June 10, 2015.

To a lesser extent, another obstacle to further enlargement is the notion that this might prompt more aggressive moves by Putin.[120] President of the EU Commission Jean-Claude Juncker ruled out any new accession during his mandate, which is set to end in 2019.[121] In spite of this, EU officials note that the prospect of membership is still the most promising lever the European Union can use on its eastern partners.[122] French officials agreed that the European Union has few options on the table besides integration.[123] One such option is a visa agreement between aspiring members and the European Union. Such discussions have made progress in the cases of Georgia and Moldova, while they are being stalled with Russia.[124]

In November 2015, a review of the ENP put greater emphasis on differentiation—a concept that outlines the need to provide different EU partners with different incentives and measures.[125] The Ukraine crisis may prompt changes at a more technical level, such as a revision of what the European Neighborhood Instrument—the ENP fund that amounts to 15.4 billion euros for the period 2014–2020[126]—can be used for, to include security and defense in addition to development

---

[120] Interview with EU official, June 10, 2015.

[121] "Juncker to Halt Enlargement as EU Commission Head," *EUBusiness*, July 15, 2014.

[122] Interview with EU official, June 3, 2015.

[123] Interview with French officials, June 18, 2015.

[124] Interview with French officials, June 18, 2015.

[125] European Commission, *Joint Communication to the European Parliament, the Council, the European Economic and Social Committee and the Committee of the Regions: Review of the European Neighbourhood Policy*, JOIN(2015) 50 final, Brussels, November 18, 2015. On differentiation, the EEAS further notes that

> While the underlying principles and objectives of the ENP apply to all partners, the EU's relationship with each one of its partners is unique, and the instruments of the ENP are tailored to serve each of those relationships. The ENP provides the EU with a toolbox of instruments that allows it to adapt and differentiate its policy, in line with the different developments, ambitions and needs of its partners" (EEAS, "European Neighborhood Policy [ENP]," fact sheet, undated[b]).

[126] European Commission, "Towards a New European Neighbourhood Policy: The EU Launches a Consultation on the Future of its Relations with Neighbouring Countries," press release, March 4, 2015.

assistance. There is an increasing realization that the meaning of security has changed, and threats have become more hybrid, a development that may require the European Union to adapt its existing tools accordingly.[127]

---

[127] Interview with EU official, June 17, 2015.

CHAPTER FIVE

Conclusion

Most European countries have imposed sanctions that, in combination with other factors, have driven Russia into recession and constrained future growth prospects. They have shifted resources to buttressing Ukraine economically and supporting its reform efforts. Several countries have increased their defense spending; others have halted planned declines. The United States is also showing the lead by more than quadrupling the funds devoted to the European Reassurance Initiative in its fiscal year 2017 defense budget.

The various scenarios and contingencies that we heard in Sweden, Estonia, Latvia, and Poland concerning Russian actions and potential NATO reactions need to be assessed by the U.S. Department of Defense (DoD). This refers to

- a serious look at Russian capabilities to politically subvert a Baltic State, including by seizing a border enclave or fomenting internal unrest. DoD could use political-military games to understand the potential Alliance difficulties in reaching consensus, the options open to NATO, and the time required. More detailed analysis of the Baltic internal security forces would also be valuable.
- a better understanding of the Russian ability to prevent reinforcement to the Baltic States; DoD could subject some of the "unusual" scenarios, such as the seizure of Gotland, to modeling and simulation. Similarly, for sustained air operations over the Baltic States, how important does access to Swedish (and possibly Finnish) airspace become?

- a clear view of the role that Kaliningrad might play, with its strong antiair defenses; how would NATO neutralize it? The whole topic of neutralization of Kaliningrad brings up the issue of escalation and potential Russian response to what Russia would see as strikes on the Russian homeland
- support for improving intelligence sharing and decisionmaking within NATO, especially with regard to indicators and warnings of Russian activity.
- looming above all of this, the nuclear issue. How can escalation be controlled, and what would be the levers available?

Here again, NATO's adaptation will play a key role in mitigating some of these threats. This adaptation—as seen through the results of the 2014 Wales and 2016 Warsaw Summits—is generally consensual, unlike other measures such as the provision of lethal aid to Ukraine or the prepositioning of troops in the Baltic States, which continue to divide Europeans. Tensions with Russia are also an opportunity, in the sense that reassurance measures help maintain interoperability gains between NATO partners after withdrawal from Afghanistan. Support for NATO membership is also increasing in Sweden and Finland.

Basically, the ball is now in Russia's court. If Moscow deescalates the Ukraine crisis or even does not further increase fighting levels, most European governments will be sympathetic to some relaxation of sanctions. If, on the other hand, Russia escalates its involvement in Ukraine or threatens aggressive steps elsewhere, the debate in Europe about a further response will be renewed. Russia may also be playing for time, knowing that there is a clear geographical divide between countries bordering Russia and others on how real and immediate the Russian threat is, and the migration crisis is pushing concerns about Russian threats even further into the background for numerous European countries. The threat of international and domestic terrorism, the Syrian and Libyan civil wars, and the unprecedented flood of refugees are all powerful distractions that tend to dominate the concerns of all but Russia's closest neighbors. Nevertheless, the Ukraine crisis has caused a refocus within the Alliance on the defense of NATO territory for the first time in more than 20 years. This refocus should continue to yield gradual improvements in the Alliance's defensive capabilities, even as the prospects for concerted Western action in distant out-of-area contingencies continue to diminish.

List of Interviews

Table A.1
Interviews

Location	Number of Interviews	Type of Organization (number of interviewees)
Belgium (Brussels, Mons)	17	EEAS (9[a]); European Parliament official (1); NATO International Staff officials (14); NATO country officials (2)
Estonia (Tallinn, Narva)	5	Ministry of Defense (2); Ministry of Foreign affairs (2); research organizations (2); academia (1); foreign officials (2)
France (Paris)	7	Ministry of Defense (3); Ministry of Foreign affairs (2); research organizations (4)
Germany (Berlin)	4[b]	Officials (1); research organizations (4); academia (1)
Latvia (Riga)	8	Ministry of Defense (2); former government official (1); research organizations (1); foreign officials (4); foreign contractors (4); academia (1)
Poland (Warsaw)	11	Ministry of Defense (15); National Security Bureau (5); research organizations (8); former government official (1)
Sweden (Stockholm)	10	Ministry of Defense (1); Ministry of Foreign Affairs (5); Swedish Parliament (1); media (2); research organizations (2); foreign officials (1)
United States (Washington, D.C., and Arlington, Va.)	6	Foreign officials (9)

[a] Includes one phone interview.

[b] Additional discussions in Berlin at a conference on "Hybrid Warfare" with German and foreign officials and analysts.

In a few instances, this study also draws from interviews conducted in Ukraine for other RAND studies between April and August 2015.

Guidelines for Interviews

Interviews were open-ended, with these questions acting as a general guide.

Strategic environment
1) Can you describe your country's/EU's/NATO's relationship with Russia pre–March 2014?
2) Can you describe your country's/EU's/NATO's relationship with Russia today?
3) What makes Russia important to your country's/EU's/NATO's foreign policy interests?

Threat perceptions
4) What are the most important security issues facing your country/EU/NATO today and why?
5) What do you see as the top threats from Russia? How do you see the Russian threat evolving?
6) What do you think are the right tools and institutions to prepare for and remedy these threats?
7) What aspects of this crisis make it a military issue for your country/EU/NATO (if at all)?
8) What aspects of this crisis make it a domestic policy issue for your country (if at all)?
   a. Is there a popular movement in your country that supports Russia's position on the Ukraine issue?
   b. Does Russia have the ability to influence your country's civil society (public opinion, media, academia, etc.)?
   c. Are there cleavages within your country that Rus-

sia or others might seek to exploit? How deep are these cleavages? What could be national or regional responses to address these cleavages?

9) What aspects of this crisis make it an economic and financial issue for your country (if at all)?

10) What aspects of this crisis make it an energy Issue for your country (if at all)?

11) Are your concerns with regard to the Russian crisis similar to those of your allies and partners? If not, what are some differences?

12) Do EU/NATO countries share similar concerns with regard to the crisis with Russia? If not, what are some differences?

Responding to the threat

13) What actions has your country/EU/NATO taken to mitigate the issues you just described?

14) What have been the political and economic implications of these actions for your country/EU/NATO?

15) How long do you expect you will need to pursue these actions for?

16) How do you see European states cooperating, or not, in the face of common challenges and threats? What about challenges and threats that are more specific to your country?

17) How do you see the current threat environment affecting defense spending and priorities in your country? Among partner countries?

18) How may the current crisis impact the future of European security? Of NATO's security?

19) What would be the right tools at the EU/NATO level to prepare for and remedy these threats?

20) What move(s) from Russia would warrant further actions from your country/EU/NATO (i.e., what "red lines" would Russia have to cross)? If Russia made these moves . . .

    a. What types of action would your country take unilaterally?

    b. What types of action would your country advocate for within the EU?

    c. What types of action would your country advocate within NATO?

Reshaping engagement policy
Engagement with Russia

21) How has the Ukrainian crisis changed your country's/EU's/ NATO's engagement policy with Russia?
22) How do you see this relationship evolving in the next six month to one year?
23) What would need to happen for your country's/EU's/NATO's relation with Russia to normalize?

Neighborhood policy

24) How has the Ukrainian crisis impacted your country's relationship with other EU countries *[when country is a member of the EU]*?
   a. Do you expect these relationships to experience more changes, and if so, under what circumstances might this happen?
25) How has the Ukrainian crisis impacted your country's relationship with other NATO countries *[when country is a member of NATO]*?
   a. Do you expect these relationships to experience more changes, and if so, under what circumstances might this happen?
26) How has the Ukrainian crisis impacted your country's relationship with non-NATO European countries (Sweden, Finland, Belarus, Ukraine, Moldova)?
   a. Do you expect these relationships to experience more changes, and if so, under what circumstances might this happen?
27) How has the Ukrainian crisis impacted your country's relationship with non-NATO, non-European countries on Russia's periphery (Georgia, Armenia, Azerbaijan, Uzbekistan, Kyrgyzstan, Kazakhstan, Turkmenistan, Tajikistan)?
   a. Do you expect these relationships to experience more changes, and if so, under what circumstances might this happen?
28) How has the Ukrainian crisis impacted the EU's/NATO's relationship with non-EU countries on Russia's periphery?
   a. Do you expect these relationships to experience more changes, and if so, under what circumstances might this

happen?

29) Do you envision greater or lesser political, military, economic, or other integration in Europe going forward? How do you think this might play out?

Relationship with the United States

30) How do you see the U.S. role in Europe, politically and militarily?

31) Do you expect this role to change over time, and if so, how?

References

Adamowski, Jaroslaw, "Latvia, Lithuania to Raise Defense Spending," *Defense News*, July 30, 2015. As of October 23, 2015:
http://www.dcfensenews.com/story/defense/international/europe/2015/07/29/latvia-lithuania-raise-defense-spending/30843863/

———, "NATO Agrees on E European Rotational Troops at Warsaw Summit," *Defense News*, July 8, 2016. As of August 19, 2016:
http://www.defensenews.com/story/defense/omr/roadtowarsaw/2016/07/08/nato-agrees-eastern-european-rotational-battalions-warsaw-summit/86863516/

"Après les Attentats, le Budget 2016 Prévoit 815 Millions d'Euros pour les Mesures de Sécurité," *Le Monde*, November 30, 2015.

Archick, Kristin, "The European Union: Questions and Answers," Congressional Research Service, January 19, 2016.

Aschehoug, Andrew-Sebastien, "Les Poupées Russes de la Propagande de Poutine en France," *Slate.fr*, February 11, 2015.

Assemblée Nationale, hearing of General Christophe Gomart, Commission de la Défense Nationale et des Forces Armées, Briefing No. 49, March 25, 2015. As of October 23, 2015:
http://www.assemblee-nationale.fr/14/cr-cdef/14-15/c1415049.asp#P3_69

"Audio: Hybride Kriegführung—'Vielmehr als ein Hype,'" German Ministry of Defense website, August 4, 2015. As of October 23, 2015:
http://www.bmvg.de/portal/a/bmvg/!ut/p/c4/NYu5CsMwEAX_SCvhQI4uwk1aN47d6UJZ0GHkld3k4yMVeQPTDA9WaCR1oFeEOakAb-1gMPvTJdDw8Ox3uu67mw2INhNFZVDD3k3XM5OSom1wibPZFUS5sy4V-CL7WUVhhaWLgYJRf8P_G9r4OcbpfrML7kBFuMzx9mEHBT/

"B-52 Bombers to Exercise over Sweden," Radio Sweden, May 20, 2015. As of October 23, 2015:
http://sverigesradio.se/sida/artikel.aspx?programid=2054&artikel=6170058

Balzli, Beat, Christoph B. Schiltz, and André Tauber, "Halten Sie sich an Frau Merkel. Ich Mache das!" *Die Welt*, March 8, 2015. As of October 23, 2015: http://www.welt.de/politik/ausland/article138178098/Halten-Sie-sich-an-Frau-Merkel-Ich-mache-das.html

"Belarus Says Does Not Need a Russian Military Base: Report," Reuters, October 6, 2015.

Birnbaum, Michael, "A Year into a Conflict with Russia, Are Sanctions Working?" *Washington Post*, March 27, 2015.

Central Intelligence Agency, *World Factbook*, website, undated. As of October 23, 2015: https://www.cia.gov/library/publications/the-world-factbook/wfbExt/region_eur.html

Christie, Edward Hunter, "Sanctions After Crimea: Have They Worked?" *NATO Review*, undated. As of October 23, 2015: http://www.nato.int/docu/Review/2015/Russia/sanctions-after-crimea-have-they-worked/EN/index.htm

CIA—*See* Central Intelligence Agency.

Clifton, Jon, "Russia Receives Lowest Approval in World; U.S. Highest," Gallup website, April 21, 2015. As of October 23, 2015: http://www.gallup.com/poll/182795/russia-receives-lowest-approval-world-highest.aspx

Conley, Heather A., Theodore P. Gerber, Lucy Moore, and Mihaela David, "Russian Soft Power in the 21st Century: An Examination of Russian Compatriot Policy in Estonia," Center for Strategic and International Studies, August 2011.

de Larrinaga, Nicholas, "NATO's Tripled Baltic Air Policing Mission Begins," *Jane's Defence Weekly*, April 30, 2014.

Dempsey, Judy, "Time to End the EU-NATO Standoff," *Strategic Europe* blog, Carnegie Europe, December 8, 2014. As of October 23, 2015: http://carnegieeurope.eu/strategiceurope/?fa=57423

"Déploiement d'un Détachement de Chars Leclerc à Drawsko," press release, French Embassy in Warsaw, updated May 8, 2015. As of October 23, 2015: http://www.ambafrance-pl.org/Deploiement-d-un-detachement-de-chars-Leclerc-a-Drawsko

Directorate General for International Cooperation and Development, "The Instrument contributing to Stability and Peace (IcSP)," Brussels, European Commission, undated. As of October 25, 2015: https://ec.europa.eu/europeaid/sectors/human-rights-and-governance/peace-and-security/instrument-contributing-stability-and-peace_en

Dreyer, Ina, and Nicu Popescu, "Do Sanctions Against Russia Work?" European Union Institute for Security Studies, Brief Issue No. 35, December 2014.

Duxbury, Charlie, "Sweden Plans to Increase Military Spending," *Wall Street Journal*, March 12, 2015. As of October 23, 2015:
http://www.wsj.com/articles/
sweden-plans-to-increase-military-spending-1426198507

EEAS—*See* European External Action Service.

Emmott, Robin, and Gabriela Baczynska, "Italy, Hungary Say No Automatic Renewal of Russia Sanctions," Reuters, March 14, 2016.

EU Naval Force Somalia, "Countering Piracy off the Coast of Somalia," fact sheet, undated. As of October 23, 2015:
http://eunavfor.eu/home/about-us

European Commission, "Towards a New European Neighbourhood Policy: The EU Launches a Consultation on the Future of its Relations with Neighbouring Countries," press release, March 4, 2015. As of October 23, 2015:
http://europa.eu/rapid/press-release_IP-15-4548_en.htm

———, *Joint Communication to the European Parliament, the Council, the European Economic and Social Committee and the Committee of the Regions: Review of the European Neighbourhood Policy*, JOIN(2015) 50 final, Brussels, November 18, 2015. As of September 13, 2016:
https://eeas.europa.eu/enp/
documents/2015/151118_joint-communication_review-of-the-enp_en.pdf

European Commission and High Representative of the European Union for Foreign Affairs and Security Policy, "Capacity Building in Support of Security and Development—Enabling Partners to Prevent and Manage Crises," Joint Communication to the European Parliament and the Council JOIN(2015) 17, Brussels, April 28, 2015. As of October 25, 2015:
http://eur-lex.europa.eu/legal-content/EN/TXT/PDF/?uri=CELEX:52015JC0017
&from=EN

European External Action Service, "EUAM Ukraine," EEAS web page, undated(a). As of October 25, 2015:
http://www.eeas.europa.eu/csdp/missions-and-operations/euam-ukraine/
index_en.htm

———, "European Neighborhood Policy (ENP)," fact sheet, undated(b). As of October 25, 2015:
http://eeas.europa.eu/enp/about-us/index_en.htm

———, "Common Security and Defence Policy: EU Integrated Border Assistance Mission in Libya (EUBAM Libya)," fact sheet, January 2015.

Evans, Stephen, "Germans Not Keen to Ruffle Russian Feathers," *BBC News* magazine, April 12, 2014.

Fabius, Laurent, "La Politique Étrangère de la France: Quelle Autonomie pour Quelle Ambition?" speech before the French Senate, October 15, 2015. As of October 25, 2015:
http://www.diplomatie.gouv.fr/fr/le-ministere-et-son-reseau/maedi-une-diplomatie-globale-au-21eme-siecle/la-politique-etrangere-de-la-france-quelle-autonomie-pour-quelle-ambition/article/la-politique-etrangere-de-la-france-quelle-autonomie-pour-quelle-ambition

"Face à la Russie, Jean-Claude Juncker Veut une armée Européenne," *L'Express* and Agence France-Presse, March 8, 2015. As of October 25, 2015:
http://www.lexpress.fr/actualite/monde/europe/face-a-la-russie-jean-claude-juncker-veut-une-armee-europeenne_1659168.html

Farmer, Ben, and David Blair, "Estonia Stages Biggest Military Exercise in Country's History amid Fears of Russian 'Aggression,'" *Telegraph*, May 12, 2015. As of October 25, 2015:
http://www.telegraph.co.uk/news/worldnews/europe/estonia/11600458/Estonia-stages-biggest-military-exercise-in-countrys-history-amid-fears-of-Russian-aggression.html

"Finland and Sweden Sign Memorandum of Understanding with NATO," press release, NATO Supreme Headquarters Allied Powers Europe Public Affairs Office, September 5, 2014. As of October 23, 2015:
http://www.aco.nato.int/finland-and-sweden-signing-a-memorandum-of-understanding-with-nato-for-operational-and-logistic-support.aspx

"Finnmark Celebrates 70-Year Liberation Anniversary," *Norway Post*, October 22, 2014. As of September 18, 2016:
http://www.norwaypost.no/news-politics/30251-

Ford, Matt, "After Crimea, Sweden Flirts with Joining NATO," *Atlantic*, March 12, 2014. As of October 25, 2015:
http://www.theatlantic.com/international/archive/2014/03/after-crimea-sweden-flirts-with-joining-nato/284362/

Galeotti, Mark, "The 'Gerasmiov Doctrine' and Russian Non-Linear War," blog post, *In Moscow's Shadows*, July 6, 2014. As of September 18, 2016:
https://inmoscowsshadows.wordpress.com/2014/07/06/the-gerasimov-doctrine-and-russian-non-linear-war/

"Germany and Russia: How Very Understanding," *Economist*, May 10, 2014.

Gibbs, Walter, "Russia and Norway Reach Accord on Barents Sea," *New York Times*, April 27, 2010.

Giegerich, Bastian, "Workshop Report: Perspectives on Hybrid Warfare," *IISS Voices*, International Institute for Strategic Studies, July 1, 2015. As of October 23, 2015:
https://www.iiss.org/en/iiss%20voices/blogsections/iiss-voices-2015-dda3/july-2632/perspectives-on-hybrid-warfare-cd5e

Higgins, Andrew, "Norway Reverts to Cold War Mode as Russian Air Patrols Spike," *New York Times*, April 1, 2015. As of October 23, 2015: http://www.nytimes.com/2015/04/02/world/europe/a-newly-assertive-russia-jolts-norways-air-defenses-into-action.html?_r=0

————, "Latvian Region Has Distinct Identity, and Allure for Russia," *New York Times*, May 20, 2015.

Hoffman, Frank, "On Not-So-New Warfare: Political Warfare vs. Hybrid Threats," *War on the Rocks*, July 28, 2014.

Infratest dimap, ARD-DeutschlandTREND, survey report, October 2014.

Johnson, Simon, "Sweden Intercepts Russian Military Planes Flying with Their Transponders Off over Baltic Region," Reuters, March 24, 2015. As of October 23, 2015: http://www.businessinsider.com/r-sweden-intercepts-russian-planes-over-baltic-amid-regional-tensions-2015-3

Jones, Bruce, "Russia Place 38,000 Troops on Alert for Snap Exercises," *Jane's Defence Weekly*, March 16, 2015.

"Juncker to Halt Enlargement as EU Commission Head," *EUBusiness*, July 15, 2014. As of October 23, 2015: http://www.eubusiness.com/news-eu/politics-juncker.x29

Kamp, Karl-Heinz, "NATO-EU Cooperation: Forget It!" *Strategic Europe* blog, Carnegie Europe, October 30, 2013.

Kanter, James, "E.U. to Extend Sanctions Against Russia, but Divisions Show," *New York Times*, December 18, 2015.

Karmanau, Yaras, "Putin Moves to Establish Russian Military Base in Belarus," Associated Press, September 19, 2015.

Kofman, Michael, Katya Migacheva, Brian Nichiporuk, Andrew Radin, Olesya Tkacheva, and Jenny Oberholtzer, "Lessons from Russia's Operations in Crimea and Eastern Ukraine," Santa Monica, Calif.: RAND Corporation, RR-1498-A, 2017.

LaGrone, Sam, "Finns Drop Depth Charges Against 'Possible Underwater Object' near Helsinki," *U.S. Naval Institute News*, April 28, 2015. As of October 25, 2015: http://news.usni.org/2015/04/28/finns-drop-depth-charges-against-possible-underwater-object-near-helsinki

Larrabee, F. Stephen, Stephanie Pezard, Andrew Radin, Nathan A. Chandler, Keith W. Crane, and Thomas S. Szayna, *Russia and the West After the Ukrainian Crisis: European Vulnerabilities to Russian Pressures*, Santa Monica, Calif.: RAND Corporation, RR-1305-A, 2017.

"Latvia," *Jane's World's Armies*, July 2015.

Levintova, Ekaterina, "Good Neighbours? Dominant Narratives About the 'Other' in Contemporary Polish and Russian Newspapers," *Europe-Asia Studies*, Vol. 62, No. 8, 2010, pp. 1339–1361.

Lindblad, Erik, "The Future of Sweden's Partnership with NATO," paper, Sciences-Po (Paris School of International Affairs) and Institut de Recherche Stratégique de l'Ecole Militaire, Spring 2014. As of October 25, 2015: http://www.sciencespo.fr/psia/sites/sciencespo.fr.psia/files/LINDBLAD_Erik_2014_IRSEM_PSIA_Prize.pdf

Major, Claudia, and Christian Mölling, "A Hybrid Security Policy for Europe: Resilience, Deterrence, and Defense as Leitmotifs," *Stiftung Wissenschaft und Politik* Comments, Vol. 22, German Institute for International and Security Affairs, April 2015. As of October 25, 2015: http://www.swp-berlin.org/fileadmin/contents/products/comments/2015C22_mjr_mlg.pdf

Merchet, Jean-Dominique, "Ukraine: Les Français Ont une Vision 'Plus Mitigée' que l'Otan," Blog Secret Défense, *L'Opinion*, August 29, 2014.

———, "Une Délégation de Parlementaires Français se Rend en Crimée," *L'Opinion*, July 22, 2015, updated July 27, 2015. As of October 25, 2015 : http://www.lopinion.fr/22-juillet-2015/delegation-parlementaires-francais-se-rend-en-crimee-26442

Merkel, Angela, Speech by Federal Chancellor on the Occasion of the 51st Munich Security Conference, Munich, February 7, 2015. As of October 25, 2015: http://www.bundesregierung.de/Content/EN/Reden/2015/2015-02-07-merkel-sicherheitskonferenz_en.html

"Merkel Toughens Up," *Economist*, November 19, 2014.

NATO—*See* North Atlantic Treaty Organization.

NATO Defence and Security Committee, "The Readiness Action Plan: Assurance and Deterrence for the Post-2014 Security Environment," NATO Parliamentary Assembly, April 16, 2015.

"NATO Halves Baltic Air Policing Mission," Agence France-Presse, August 4, 2015. As of October 23, 2015: http://www.defensenews.com/story/defense/international/europe/2015/08/04/nato-halves-baltic-air-policing-mission/31139949/

"NATO's Practical Support to Ukraine," fact sheet, North Atlantic Treaty Organization, June 2015. As of October 25, 2015: http://www.nato.int/nato_static_fl2014/assets/pdf/pdf_2015_06/20150624_1506-Factsheet_PracticalSupportUkraine_en.pdf

Neukirch, Ralf, "Is Germany a Country of Russia Apologists?" *Spiegel*, March 31, 2014.

Neumann, Peter R., "Foreign Fighters Total in Syria/Iraq Now Exceeds 20,000; Surpasses Afghanistan Conflict in the 1980s," London: International Centre for the Study of Radicalisation, January 26, 2015. As of October 23, 2015: http://icsr.info/2015/01/foreign-fighter-total-syriairaq-now-exceeds-20000-surpasses-afghanistan-conflict-1980s/

Noack, Rick, "Why Do Nearly 40 Percent of Germans Endorse Russia's Annexation of Crimea?" *Washington Post*, November 28, 2014.

North Atlantic Treaty Organization, "Founding Act on Mutual Relations, Cooperation and Security Between NATO and the Russian Federation," May 1997. As of October 23, 2015: http://www.nato.int/cps/en/natohq/official_texts_25468.htm

———, *Wales Summit Declaration*, September 5, 2014. As of October 25, 2015: http://www.nato.int/cps/en/natohq/official_texts_112964.htm

———, "NATO Publishes Defence Expenditures Data for 2014 and Estimates for 2015: Financial and Economic Data Relating to NATO Defence," press release PR/CP(2015) 093-COR1, June 22, 2015. As of October 25, 2015: http://www.nato.int/nato_static_fl2014/assets/pdf/pdf_2015_06/20150622_PR_CP_2015_093-v2.pdf

———, *Warsaw Summit Communiqué,* July 9, 2016. As of August 24, 2016: http://www.nato.int/cps/en/natohq/official_texts_133169.htm

"Norway Kicked Russian Patrol Vessels out of Spitsbergen," *Barents Observer*, May 27, 2008.

Norwegian Ministry of Foreign Affairs, "Norway's Arctic Policy," 2015.

Ochmanek, David, Andrew R. Hoehn, James T. Quinlivan, Seth G. Jones, and Edward L. Warner, *America's Security Deficit: Addressing the Imbalance Between Strategy and Resources in a Turbulent World*, Santa Monica, Calif.: RAND Corporation, RB-9870-RC, 2015. As of October 23, 2015: http://www.rand.org/pubs/research_reports/RR1223.html

O'Dwyer, Gerard, "Norway, Russia Strengthen Relations," *Defense News*, April 4, 2012.

———, "Russia Warns Sweden and Finland Against NATO Membership," *Defense News*, June 12, 2014. As of October 23, 2015: http://www.defensenews.com/article/20140612/DEFREG01/306120040/Russia-Warns-Sweden-Finland-Against-NATO-Membership

———, "Sweden and Finland Pursue 'Special Relationship' with NATO," *Defense News,* October 10, 2014.

———, "Sweden Proposes Aggressive Nordic Defense," *Defense News*, February 10, 2015a. As of October 23, 2015:
http://www.defensenews.com/story/defense/policy-budget/warfare/2015/02/10/
sweden-nordic-cooperation-russia-nordefco-cooperation-nbg--sreide-battlegroup/
22865811/

———, "New Poll Shows Sharp Shift in NATO Support," *Defense News*, September 17, 2015b.

———, "9.8% Budget Hike Set for Norwegian Armed Forces," *Defense News*, October 9, 2015c.

Philippot, Damien, and Esteban Pratviel, "Les Français, la Perception du Conflit Ukraino-Russe et la Livraison de Navires de Guerre à la Russie," poll of the Institut Français d'Opinion Publique for *La Tribune*, January 2015. As of October 23, 2015:
http://www.ifop.com/media/poll/2912-1-study_file.pdf

"Poll Shows More Swedes in Favor of NATO for First Time," Reuters, October 29, 2014. As of October 23, 2015:
http://www.reuters.com/article/2014/10/29/
us-sweden-nato-idUSKBN0II1XN20141029

Pond, Elizabeth, "Secrets of the Baltic: Swedish Cold War Neutrality Revisited," *World Policy* blog, September 26, 2012. As of October 23, 2015:
http://www.worldpolicy.org/blog/2012/09/26/
secrets-baltic-swedish-cold-war-neutrality-revisited

"Remarks by President Donald Tusk After the First Session of the European Council Meeting," Brussels, European Council, March 19, 2015. As of October 25, 2015:
http://www.consilium.europa.eu/en/press/
press-releases/2015/03/19-european-council-intermediate-remarks-tusk/

Rettman, Andrew, "EU 'Civilian' Mission Training Paramilitaries in Libya," *EUObserver*, November 18, 2013.

Rottem, Svein Vigeland, "The Political Architecture of Security in the Arctic—The Case of Norway," *Arctic Review on Law and Politics*, Vol. 4, No. 2, 2013.

"Russia Examines 1991 Recognition of Baltic Independence," BBC News, June 30, 2015. As of October 23, 2015:
http://www.bbc.com/news/world-europe-33325842

"Russia-Norway Tensions at Liberation Ceremony," *Local*, October 25, 2014. As of October 23, 2015:
http://www.thelocal.no/20141025/russia-norway-tensions-at-liberation-celebration

Shevel, Oxana, "The Politics of Citizenship Policy in Post-Soviet Russia," *Post-Soviet Affairs*, Vol. 28, No. 1, 2012.

Shlapak, David A., and Michael Johnson, *Reinforcing Deterrence on NATO's Eastern Flank: Wargaming the Defense of the Baltics*, Santa Monica, Calif.: RAND Corporation, RR-1253-A, 2016. As of September 8, 2016:
http://www.rand.org/pubs/research_reports/RR1253.html

Simmons, Katie, Bruce Stokes, and Jacob Poushter, "NATO Publics Blame Russia for Ukrainian Crisis, but Reluctant to Provide Military Aid," Pew Research Center, June 10, 2015.

SIPRI—*See* Stockholm International Peace Research Institute.

Smith-Windsor, Brooke, "Putting the 'N' Back in NATO: A High North Policy Framework for the Atlantic Alliance?" NATO Research Paper No. 94, July 2013.

Stockholm International Peace Research Institute, "Regional Coverage," database, undated. As of October 23, 2015:
http://www.sipri.org/research/armaments/milex/milex_database/regional_coverage

———, "Trends in World Military Expenditure 2014," fact sheet, April 2015.

Sverdrup, Ulf, and Elana Wilson Rowe, "Norway Is Re-Thinking Its Russian Relations," *Europe's World*, Summer 2015. As of October 23, 2015:
http://europesworld.org/2015/07/14/norway-re-thinking-russian-relations/#.VuxT42f2aM8

"Swedish Defense Bill 2016–2020," Government Offices of Sweden, April 24, 2015. As of October 23, 2015:
http://www.government.se/government-policy/defence/the-swedish-defence-bill-2016-2020/

Tardy, Thierry, "Enabling Partners to Manage Crises: From 'Train and Equip' to Capacity-Building," European Union Institute for Security Studies Brief, Issue No. 18, June 2015.

"Timeline—EU Restrictive Measures in Response to the Crisis in Ukraine," Brussels, European Council, undated. As of October 23, 2015:
http://www.consilium.europa.eu/en/policies/sanctions/ukraine-crisis/history-ukraine-crisis/

Troianovski, Anton, "Germany Seeks to Counter Russian 'Propaganda' in the Baltics," *Wall Street Journal*, April 17, 2015.

"Ukraine/Macro-Financial Assistance," Brussels, European Commission, updated July 22, 2015. As of October 23, 2015:
http://ec.europa.eu/economy_finance/international/neighbourhood_policy/ukraine_en.htm

U.S. Energy Information Administration, "Norway," database, updated April 28, 2014. As of October 23, 2015:
http://www.eia.gov/countries/cab.cfm?fips=no

Van Puyvelde, Damien, "Hybrid War—Does It Even Exist?" *NATO Review*, 2015. As of November 29, 2015: http://www.nato.int/docu/review/2015/Also-in-2015/hybrid-modern-future-warfare-russia-ukraine/EN/index.htm

Vandiver, John, "NATO: Fewer Flights Needed to Patrol Baltic Airspace," *Stars and Stripes*, August 5, 2015.

Wade, Jonathan, "Norway-Led Arctic Challenge Exercise 2015 Starts," Sentinel Analytical Group, May 25, 2015. As of October 23, 2015: http://thesentinel.ca/norway-led-arctic-challenge-exercise-2015-starts/

Wike, Richard, Bruce Stokes, and Jacob Poushter, "Global Public Back U.S. on Fighting ISIS, But Are Critical of Post-9/11 Torture," comment on Pew Research Center Spring 2015 *Global Attitudes Survey*, June 23, 2015. As of October 23, 2015: http://www.pewglobal.org/2015/06/23/1-americas-global-image/

Winnerstig, Mike, ed., "Tools of Destabilization: Russian Soft Power and Non-Military Influence in the Baltic States," Sweden Defense Research Agency, December 16, 2014. As of October 23, 2015: http://www.foi.se/rapport?rNo=FOI-R--3990--SE

Zevelev, Igor, "Russia's Policy Toward Compatriots in the Former Soviet Union," *Russia in Global Affairs*, Vol. 6, No. 1, January–March 2008.